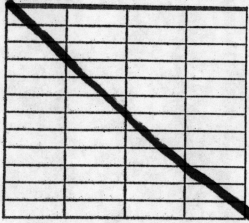

The Uses and Misuses of Tests

Examining Current Issues in Educational and Psychological Testing

Charles W. Daves, EDITOR

Foreword by Gregory R. Anrig

The Uses and Misuses of Tests

 Jossey-Bass Publishers

San Francisco • Washington • London • 1984

THE USES AND MISUSES OF TESTS
Examining Current Issues in Educational and Psychological Testing
by Charles W. Daves, Editor

Copyright © 1984 by: Jossey-Bass Inc., Publishers
433 California Street
San Francisco, California 94104
&
Jossey-Bass Limited
28 Banner Street
London EC1Y 8QE

Library of Congress Cataloging in Publication Data
Main entry under title:

The Uses and misuses of tests.

(The Jossey-Bass social and behavioral science
series) (The Jossey-Bass higher education series)
Includes bibliographies and index.
1. Educational tests and measurements—United
States—Evaluation—Addresses, essays, lectures.
2. Educational tests and measurements—Social aspects—
United States—Addresses, essays, lectures. I. Daves,
Charles W. II. Series. III. Series: Jossey-Bass
higher education series.
LB3051.U84   1984   371.2'6   84-47982
ISBN 0-87589-614-6

Manufactured in the United States of America

The paper in this book meets the guidelines for
permanence and durability of the Committee on
Production Guidelines for Book Longevity of the
Council on Library Resources.

JACKET DESIGN BY WILLI BAUM

FIRST EDITION

Code 8429

A joint publication in
The Jossey-Bass
Social and Behavioral Science Series
and
The Jossey-Bass
Higher Education Series

Consulting Editor
Testing and Measurement

Jayjia Hsia
Educational Testing Service

Foreword

In recent years, the matter of test use and misuse has been in the forefront of discussion by educators and the public in general, in the press, and in scholarly journals. In 1983, several reports by blue-ribbon commissions and panels were issued, giving education attention rivaled only by that of the post-Sputnik years. In 1983 and 1984, professional associations and individuals in the psychological community vigorously reviewed the third and fourth drafts of the *Joint Technical Standards for Educational and Psychological Testing.* In this milieu, heightened interest has been given to fair and appropriate use of educational and psychological testing as a tool for decision making in our society. Critics, many with good reason, question the role of current assessment instruments for school and college admission and placement, competency testing, and job selection, licensing, and certification—as applied to individuals and groups.

The 1983 Educational Testing Service (ETS) Invitational Conference, titled *The Uses and Misuses of Tests,* was designed to shed light on this critical and timely topic and extend our understanding about fair and appropriate test use in a variety of applications. The chapters in this work address the four major centers of interest developed in the conference: the public stake in proper test use (Chapter One), professional standards for proper test use (Chapters Two and Three), issues in test use in schools (Chapters Four and Five) and in higher education (Chapters Six and Seven), and test use and the law (Chapter Eight).

In the opening chapter, John Casteen asserts that "proper tests properly used" will continue to assist in the process of learning and the verification of competence. Measurement specialists can contribute to state and national efforts in the improvement of education so that we will better understand the meaning of competence and develop new modes of assessment, in the public interest.

Because testing plays such a key role in American society, the development of new *Joint Technical Standards for Educational and Psychological Testing,* sponsored by the three major professional associations (American Psychological Association, American Educational Research Association, and National Council on Measurement in Education) to ensure "proper use of well-constructed and validated tests," is critical to decision making about persons and programs and the enhancement of broad and "equitable access to education and employment." Melvin Novick describes the process of standards development in Chapter Two. He is joined in debate on this topic in Chapter Three through the commentaries of Anne Anastasi, Frank Snyder, and Mary Tenopyr. The issues they address include whether one set of detailed standards can apply to highly varied needs and situations, whether the standards should represent agreed-on goals or general principles (not specified details and processes as well), and whether refined standards can be developed and established ahead of and apart from a larger plan to improve measurement in America.

Based on his experience gauging and reporting on the effectiveness of early childhood programs in New York City, former chancellor Anthony Alvarado, in Chapter Four, calls for research and development assistance from the measurement community in the difficult task of creating appropriate and practical means of accessing educational programs for the very young student. In Chapter Five, Diane Ravitch writes that despite legitimate criticisms, when used in limited fashion, "well-made standardized tests" can serve effectively as an early warning system to society and can enhance the learning process, especially by providing benchmarks on how well learning is taking place.

The usefulness of standardized test scores as supplementary information for various academic purposes is clear, asserts Fred Hargadon; the usefulness differs by institution. Because of the varied and complex educational system in this country, the misuse-of-tests issue is more complicated than often thought, an issue best explored through the development and consideration of case studies of "misuse." Franklyn Jenifer believes that standardized tests should not be viewed as the enemy of minorities in the admissions process. Instead of "killing the messenger," Jenifer advocates directing our attention to the message and identifying solutions to the problem of minority student performance. He recommends, for now, a broad set of measures to select a student body through a two-stage admissions process.

In Chapter Eight, Donald Bersoff analyzes claims, especially in court cases, that psychological tests, including minimum competency tests, used in the public schools discriminate against racial and ethnic minorities and against handicapped students and deny full realization of their rights. He blames what he terms "continuing confusion" about such tests on the judiciary and on psychologists themselves but notes that the courts, in attempting to protect the rights of test takers, have engendered greater examination of the measurement work of psychologists and prompted further work in alternative means of assessment.

It is heartening to note that persons in such key roles are sensitive to and knowledgeable about the issues of test use and misuse. They are professionals who are able to influence practice directly as well as stimulate discussion through the conference and this volume.

August 1984   Gregory R. Anrig
                                                 President
                                                 Educational Testing Service

Frederic M. Lord

Frederic M. Lord's contributions to test theory over the past four decades comprise a monumental achievement. Marked by a marvelous thematic continuity, they have led to the reconceptualization of the problems of test theory in terms of latent trait measurement. In large measure because of Lord's work, there now stands a consistent framework for understanding test properties as well as an explanatory system of enormous predictive power. Equally important, Lord pioneered the rigorous application of mathematical statistics to test theory, thereby eliminating much of the confusion and imprecision that had plagued the field since its inception.

Beginning with his psychometric monograph on *A Theory of Test Scores* in 1952, which was based on his doctoral dissertation, this line of development led to a landmark text on *Statistical Theories of Mental Test Scores* in 1968, written in collaboration with Melvin R. Novick. This book not only definitively codifies classical true score theory but also provides the mathematical foundations for a variety of new approaches to mental testing, including generalizability theory and item response theory. In 1980, his work on the latter topic having expanded and deepened, Lord published an influential volume on *Applications of Item Response Theory to Practical Testing Prob-*

lems, which provides both an integrative distillation of theory and an innovative guide to practice.

Standing out like milestones in this persistent march toward integrative theory are an impressive number of classic contributions that make their own singular mark. These include, among many others, the estimation of test properties by item and matrix sampling, the confrontation of paradoxes in statistical inference, the illumination of speed factors in tests and academic grades, the measurement of growth, and the development of "flexilevel" and tailored testing.

In psychometrics these days it is popular to make a distinction between classical test theory and modern test theory. That distinction, in reality, is a remarkable tribute by an entire scholarly field to the work of Lord. As further tribute, in recognition of his seminal contributions to psychometric theory and practice, Educational Testing Service presented its 1983 Award for Distinguished Service to Measurement to Frederic Mather Lord.

Previous Recipients of the ETS Award
for Distinguished Service to Measurement

1970 E. F. Lindquist
1971 Lee J. Cronbach
1972 Robert L. Thorndike
1973 Oscar K. Buros
1974 J. P. Guilford
1975 Harold Gulliksen
1976 Ralph Winfred Tyler
1977 Anne Anastasi
1978 John C. Flanagan
1979 Robert L. Ebel
1980 John B. Carroll
1981 Ledyard R Tucker
1982 Raymond B. Cattell

Contents

The Editor

Charles W. Daves is executive program director for graduate record examinations at Educational Testing Service, Princeton, New Jersey. He received his A.B. degree (1952) from Cornell University in American Studies, his A.M. degree (1953) from the University of Pennsylvania in American Civilization, and his Ph.D. degree (1965) from the University of Minnesota in English, specializing in the literature and history of England.

Daves' primary research interest has been in seventeenth-century English literature and testing in English and American literature and the humanities. His experience in evaluation includes membership on the Task Force on Measurement and Evaluation in English, sponsored by the National Council of Teachers of English. His interest in higher education is exhibited in membership for ten years on the Board of Trustees of Trenton State College and, for two years, on the Board of Higher Education of the State of New Jersey. He is editor of *Samuel Butler (1612-1680): Characters* (1970) and a coauthor, with Alan Purves and others, of *Common Sense and Testing in English* (1975).

Daves was director of test development for higher education at ETS in the mid-1970s. He has served on a number of task forces and committees on test use and guidelines for the testing of minorities.

Contributors

Anthony J. Alvarado is former chancellor, New York City Board of Education.

Anne Anastasi is professor emeritus of psychology, Fordham University.

Donald N. Bersoff is a partner in the law firm Ennis, Friedman, Bersoff, and Ewing, Washington, D.C., and professor, Joint J.D.-Ph.D. Program in Law and Psychology, University of Maryland Law School and Johns Hopkins University.

John T. Casteen III is secretary of education, Commonwealth of Virginia.

Fred A. Hargadon is senior vice-president of the College Board, New York City, and former dean of admissions, Stanford University.

Franklyn G. Jenifer is vice-chancellor, New Jersey Department of Higher Education.

Melvin R. Novick is professor of measurement and statistics, University of Iowa, and chair, Committee to Develop Joint Technical Standards for Educational and Psychological Testing.

Diane Ravitch is adjunct associate professor of history and education, Teachers College, Columbia University.

Frank W. Snyder is general manager, CTB/McGraw-Hill.

Mary L. Tenopyr is division manager, Employment Research, American Telephone and Telegraph Company.

The Uses and Misuses
of Tests

Examining Current Issues
in Educational
and Psychological Testing

1

The Public Stake
in Proper Test Use

John T. Casteen III

The sixteenth-century Chinese folk novel known in Arthur Waley's English translation as *Monkey* includes a story that most of us know.* The Prime Minister Wei Cheng persuaded the Tang Emperor T'sai Tsung to convene scholars from throughout China for a general examination to determine who should hold which positions of public trust. All who were learned, whether soldiers or peasants, were invited to come to the capital for the examination. A certain Ch'ên O, a poor countryman who lived with his mother, went to the capital to take the examination, and he earned the highest score in the land. For three days, Ch'ên O was applauded and led through the streets on horseback.

While on this tour, he attracted the attention of a wealthy young woman, the daughter of a powerful minister, who admired both Ch'ên O's figure on horseback and his examination score. The young woman threw down to Ch'ên O an embroidered ball, and the two fell in love (through the eyes, at a proper distance). Within minutes, Ch'ên O married the young woman amidst the sounds of twittering flutes and reed organs and (Waley's words) "a whole posse of maids and serving girls." In due course, Ch'ên O was appointed governor of a great province.

*Wu Ch'êng'ên. *Monkey*. (A. Waley, trans.) New York: Grove Press, 1958.

1

The thoughtful reader may not wholly grasp the causes of Ch'ên O's advancement to good fortune, but certainly the reader sees in the story a triumph of psychometric science and models of both objective, or dispassionate, public policy and connubial efficacy. Or does he?

Ch'ên O falls on hard times as he proceeds from the capital to his province. Crossing the Hung River, Ch'ên O falls into the company of Liu and Li, evil ferrymen of unstable tempers whom Ch'ên O had unwittingly injured in a previous incarnation, and he becomes first the victim of a vicious attack and later the hero of a complex tale of reincarnation and revenge.

Of such stuff are good sixteenth-century folk novels made.

Tests and Public Policy

My intention is to assess the public stake in proper test use. The topic matters because of several recent events in education and in the political world. It has in some sense always mattered because it touches directly on how we appraise competence, how we validate our methods of appraisal, and how we bridge the distance between credentials that attest disparate experience (work history, classroom study) and credentials that affirm ability to do something at an assessed level of competence on a specified day. All three terms in the expression matter: the public stake, proper tests, and proper use.

The episode from *Monkey* raises certain essential questions about the public interest in tests and measurement. However much we may doubt the validity of measurement in Prime Minister Wei Cheng's examination, the story of Ch'ên O contrasts qualifications assessed objectively and qualifications that defy objective assessment. How, indeed, might Wei Cheng have measured the probability that in a previous life Ch'ên O had offended a pair of malicious ferrymen who would do him in as he crossed the Hung River on his way to his new post? How might Wei Cheng's examination have predicted that, being murdered and flung deep into the Hung River, Ch'ên O would find favor with a noted buried golden carp (formerly a dragon king), float to the surface to be brought back to life and reunited with his wife, return to the capital to be awarded an even higher post in consideration of his tribulations in the Hung River, and live happily ever after?

These imponderables differ only in local color from demands commonly made of testing in recent years. To the extent that geographical or cultural displacement may underscore the difference between what the public can expect a test to do and what it cannot expect, perhaps Ch'ên O's adventures are a good place to begin looking at the current state of public policy as it touches testing.

Recent history is a microcosm of our attitudes toward measurement of human qualifications. Many Americans, including some in positions of trust in state governments, have moved from naive acceptance of tests (because they are part of the way things are) through a period of intense hostility to tests (because they are said to reflect the way things are to a degree not compatible with our social principles) to what a newly formed William Blake might call the higher acceptance of tests (because we seek salvation in a time of doubt about the quality of our schools, our teachers and students, indeed, about ourselves).

The fact is, of course, that Prime Minister Wei Cheng's examination resembles other examinations given at other times throughout recorded history. In Roman schools for orators, in the Inns of Court when Shakespeare was a boy, and in late medieval Spanish schools of science, rulers sought to identify competence for public life through tests. The results are rarely so well preserved as are those in *Monkey*, but they must have met some criteria of predictive validity. Students may have disliked them as much as students dislike tests in every place and time, but examinations themselves generally lasted as long as the civilizations that established them.

Our use of tests in America has had a diverse history. Rejecting the notion that tests gauge what people are, we have gravitated toward tests to measure what people *do*—a vastly different thing—and to identify specific competencies that can help us determine needs for remediation, for accelerated instruction in specific disciplines, or perhaps for instruction under nonstandard conditions. Our rejection of the idea that tests measure what people are, and thus that we can make labels to be used in sorting the population into discrete tracks, amounts to a denial of rigid social tracks or castes, not of tests. Despite occasional proposals to abandon tests (or grades) themselves, most people seem to believe that responsible change, especially in education, comes about in large part because of the existence and widespread use of coherent, reliable systems of measurement.

History ought to tell us that most commentators on the public interest in testing, indeed, most commentators on the public interest in education generally, have oversimplified the issues. The states accepted responsibility for public instruction not, as we were all told in school, because the U.S. Constitution is silent about schools, but because they had to for practical reasons. The Federalist papers are essentially silent about education. Madison and his collaborators overlooked education; they did not assign it to the states.

In any event, education as Madison knew it was not the business of the states. It belonged to localities, generally to those that were not organized into formal governments. The states took over the schools far later than most of us would guess, and with far less idealism and unanimity of purpose than the happy historians of American education have sometimes claimed. My own state, Virginia, which had local schools in the 1620s, developed a state system only at the turn of our century. We were not remarkable in this respect. It took a long time for Americans to accept the value of universal public education. Local and regional customs varied. What seemed appropriate in one place seemed inappropriate elsewhere. In more than one instance, factors utterly unrelated to education determined what was taught, where, and by whom.

Nor was testing seen as the affair of the states or of any other level of government. Madison and others wrote about the need to attest competence, but in the absence of a concept of systems of education they must have conceived examinations to be the business of separate schools.

So the public interest in assessing the results or consequences of education has its own complex history. Examinations have, no doubt, always existed in American schools. But examinations that attempt to assess the outcomes of education throughout the population are, I suspect, relatively recent inventions.

It matters in this regard that state-administered examinations began as efforts to replace disorder with order and to objectively assess competences for which more traditional credentials did not exist. When establishing state-supported schools in 1849, Oregon began testing prospective teachers. The reason was the constricted labor economy that came with the sudden movement westward to the coast. Candidates applied for teaching jobs, but they rarely had formal credentials from schools or colleges. Forced to hire persons without formal credentials, Oregon set examinations to determine who was qualified to teach.

More recent efforts to attest competence in labor forces have served various ends. The traditional professions, including law and medicine, established examinations when they formed self-regulatory professional associations, partly to guarantee competence, partly to keep out persons from nontraditional backgrounds (the physicians' early battles against the chiropractors are a good example) or poorly trained persons, and partly to protect their prestige. At other times, legislatures have imposed tests because of abuses or because new conditions seemed to define a public interest in attesting the competence of some class of practitioners. Waste water operators who work in nuclear power facilities, financial analysts, and behavioral scientists are examples.

Individual and Societal Interests

Public interest in measurement may or may not begin as an interest in schools and schooling. Either way, it extends beyond schooling to embrace three essential functions: diagnosing needs, benchmarking qualifications to *do,* and protecting against false credentials. Each function has a long history. A sixteenth-century Spanish document requiring tests to be used in determining admission to specialized courses of study refers to each one.

Whether restricted to school matters or considered more globally, each function exists in two frames. The first application touches the individual, whose needs and strengths require reasonably accurate assessment if effective programs of study or remediation are to be implemented, whose ability to do whatever he or she wishes to do may require attestation, and whose qualifications to be responsible for the well-being of other persons requires demonstration. Placement tests used in assessing students' readiness to satisfy the requirements of specific academic courses, the Scholastic Aptitude Test (SAT), and many licensure and occupational examinations belong to this group of tests.

The second application has to do with society itself, its range of needs and strengths, its capacity to work to sustain life and prosper, and its capacity to trust the specialists into whose hands it puts its young, its legal affairs, and human life itself. The National Assessment of Educational Progress serves this end in public policy and promises to provide increasingly useful information in the future as it undergoes refinement. Results of licensure and occupational examinations can yield analogous guidance on how to improve education if psychometricians share what the tests show about the whole population of test takers with persons responsible for training, and if educators use this information to improve courses and curricula.

Proper Tests

What of the matter of *proper* tests, as opposed to improper tests? Our current methods of testing developed slowly and by a route not many of us would care to travel again. It took a long time to develop a consensus within the community about what and how to measure. More than one early test affected to measure what people *are*, not what they *do*. More than one professional psychometrician entered the field because of concern about modes of testing that were more proscriptive than descriptive, better suited to exclusion than to inclusion and education.

Ultimately, the history of test use reflects our social history. Modern tests have come to be in an era when we have determined, sometimes by law and often by fits and starts, to assess human capacity to *do* rather than human value or intrinsic worth. Our gradual movement away from IQ tests in school placement and toward tests that identify discrete skills or bodies of knowledge as bases for further education reflects larger societal trends. Few would deny that effective schooling requires more precise assessments than IQ tests can provide or that validated diagnostic data provide sound points for beginning, not ending, education.

The progress of test use has not been linear. We have made more than our share of false starts. Minimum competency tests, for example, have rarely made a serious difference in our courses of instruction. The reasons are predictable enough. The analyzed results of minimum competency tests have rarely or never influenced curriculum. Students have passed or failed, but we have done little to build from one year's experience toward another year's educational program. The tests have generally existed outside the curriculum. By contrast, the success of the Advanced Placement Program has to do directly with the relationship between the tests and the curriculum. For all the talk about the danger that teachers will "teach to the test" (a slogan more notable for its alliteration than for its meaning), the best evidence has shown that the programs in which teaching and testing are most intimately related are our most successful recent examples of innovation and improvement.

Proper Use of Tests

Proper use of tests has been the topic of a reasonably constructive, if sometimes confused, dialogue since (for different reasons) the National Education Association (NEA) and Ralph Nader's associates became interested in tests several years ago. The issues, of course, are much older than the criticism generated by the La Valle Bill, but I think it is fair to say that these commentators performed a vital service by defining the issues eloquently and forcing the educational community to confront them. For most of us, this dialogue probably seems to have been between critics and defenders of tests themselves. Obviously, much of it was. But related dialogues took place in the political arena. In some states, including New York, the dialogue addressed how to control the use of tests, with concern primarily for individuals perceived (rightly or wrongly) as defenseless victims of a system ripe for control.

Another dialogue, involving many more states and predicting more accurately the direction of educational change, went on elsewhere, and it continues. Beginning in the mid-seventies, the Southern Regional Education Board (SREB) urged governors and legislators to institute universal tests for applicants for teaching positions and to insist that school programs be built on articulated goals with effectiveness gauged regularly and objectively. (SREB was not alone in advocating this strategy. I use SREB as my example primarily because the SREB publications *The Need for Quality* and *Meeting the Need for Quality* are widely known.) Unlike policy makers in states where control was the great issue, those in the SREB states saw testing as a means of verifying competence and making education account to the public for its performance. Of equal importance, they attempted to build more unitary programs of instruction, designed to include most or all students, not to subdivide the student population into arbitrary groups.

The condition of these debates may teach valuable lessons about the direction in which public policy is moving. States where control was the issue are now moving toward programs now in place in the SREB states. They have defined stipulations as to what is to be achieved in classrooms and (perhaps ironically) have specified that standardized tests are to be used as the principal instrument of assessment. Teacher examinations have gained new supporters in a time of concern about the social implications of incompetence in the classroom. Some states have sought to break the franchises customarily given to teachers' colleges by opening up teaching to holders of academic baccalaureate degrees who earn certificates by doing well on a test when they are hired and passing the review of veteran teachers during their first years in the classroom.

The NEA redefined its own position on tests, an action

that perhaps showed the direction of informed opinion on the need for objective assessments of competence and progress. One doubts that the NEA intended by this action to form a united front with the American Federation of Teachers (AFT), but the two organizations pursue reasonably compatible agendas on the role of tests in assessing the competence of candidates for teaching positions and in gauging progress within the curriculum.

Proper use of tests is an essential component of all of the major programs of educational reform now in place. Validated diagnostic procedures make general education work by guaranteeing that teachers have usable information on their students' entry-level competencies. These same procedures can bring about improvements in existing programs by reasserting original goals in terms of current progress.

In many educational endeavors, functional diagnosis is still to be developed. The custom of placing students in vocational and occupational programs on the basis of interest inventories and more-or-less unguided personal preference, without assessing readiness to undertake the required learning, must account for much of the confusion about technical education. So, too, must our chronic unwillingness to acknowledge that employers and others who receive our graduates have every right to require objective measures of accomplishment. Indeed, schools and students clearly benefit by providing measures when employers distrust education enough to form coalitions to force change in schools.

It is a peculiar quirk of history that yesterday's great issue is today's nonissue. Key documents—the National Commission Report, the Education Commission of the States (ECS) task force report, and others—derive from an earlier dialogue in which tests and test results were key issues. The publication in 1977 of *On Further Examination,* the College Board's panel report on why SAT scores declined in the late 1960s and early 1970s, was the first contribution to the discussion about how to guarantee reasonable levels of competence for all of our students. Congressional hearings of two or three years ago, hearings on whether and how to control or even eliminate tests, seem all but irrelevant to a nation concerned for the first time since Sputnik about the quality of learning in the schools.

Public policy, particularly the legislative and executive consensus about the public interest that sustains budgets and bodies of regulation and justifies new creations, today addresses why we have not, as states responsible for education and as a nation with a vital stake in our own competence, made a greater collective commitment to setting priorities for our schools, to identifying intended results from our investments, and to assessing regularly and comprehensively what we achieve, why, and how.

Education has a long, even honorable, history of naiveté about the force of public policy in determining the quality and relative affluence of schools and in defining the larger ends that schools serve. Public policy about education clearly suffered in the 1970s as other priorities dominated the scene. In that decade, the public schools by and large lost what higher education may have gained in public budgets, and the two sectors of education, when combined, lost ground as other functions of government gained larger shares of total public appropriations. The absence of clearly defined public policy and the distance between what happened in classrooms and what we wanted to discuss with the public pretty much guaranteed this outcome. In more than one state, we were content to hope that good intentions and personal probity would protect the schools.

The issues for the 1980s will not permit us to be defensive about fundamental accountability. It is in our favor that few school people are so nowadays. The link between continued development of valid and applicable assessment tools and school improvement on one hand and funding adequate to the job itself on the other hand is a solid one. The public interest and education's interest, following a long period of separation or confusion, have converged.

Readers of folk novels are entitled, I think, to take a certain amount of comfort, however tenuous it may be, in the outcomes of the intrigues and supernatural doings by which such novels function. The tale of Ch'en O ends well. He fathered a fine child. He overcame the evil ferrymen. He served with distinction as governor of a large province and exerted great influence for good. The Prime Minister Wei Cheng must have felt great pride in the propriety of his examination.

For our own time, propriety consists of other components than those that make *Monkey* live on after so many centuries. Proper tests for our time are tests that sustain teaching and learning without denying access on grounds other than individual ability to learn and that sustain the public interest in the competence of specialists and professionals without categorically excluding persons because of what they are, not what they do.

Proper tests properly used sustain learning and document competence. They do not replace or compete with education and training. They verify or validate what people do. To the extent that we who govern schools, who devise and implement the tests, who apply the results, and who teach constantly commit to refine the instruments and to seek new and better ways to assess needs and to understand competence, ours is a unique opportunity to predict the future condition of both education and society generally. The public interest requires nothing less.

2

Importance of
Professional Standards
for Fair and Appropriate
Test Use

Melvin R. Novick

As early as 1977, it became apparent that the 1974 *Standards for Educational and Psychological Tests* was becoming outdated because of a new awareness of issues and problems in testing. Especially important were problems in selection for employment or for admission to educational institutions, criterion-referenced testing, licensing and certification, assignment to special education classes, competency testing, computerized adaptive testing, test bias, and testing of persons with handicapping conditions. For this reason the presidents of the three sponsoring organizations, the American Psychological Association (APA), the American Educational Research Association (AERA), and the National Council on Measurement in Education (NCME), appointed a joint committee to review the 1974 *Standards*. This committee issued a report recommending revision of the *Standards* and recommending that the new *Standards* should:

1. Address issues of test use in a variety of applications;

2. Be a statement of technical requirements for sound profes-
    sional practice and not a social-action prescription;
3. Make it possible to determine the technical adequacy of
    a test, the appropriateness and propriety of specific applica-
    tions, and the reasonableness of inferences based on test
    results;
4. Require that test developers, publishers, and users collect
    and make available sufficient information to enable an in-
    dependent reviewer to determine whether applicable stan-
    dards were met;
5. Embody a strong ethical imperative, though it was under-
    stood that the *Standards* themselves would not contain
    enforcement mechanisms;
6. Recognize that all standards will not be uniformly applica-
    ble across a wide range of instruments and uses;
7. Be presented at a level such that a wide range of persons
    who work with tests or test results could use the *Stan-
    dards*;
8. Permit experimentation in the development, use, and in-
    terpretation of tests; and
9. Reflect the current level of consensus of recognized ex-
    perts.

The review committee's report served as the basis for the charge
to the Committee to Develop Joint Technical Standards for
Educational and Psychological Testing appointed by the three
association presidents. That committee is now in its third year
of operation. A third draft of the new *Standards* has been widely reviewed, and a fourth draft was released in February 1984.

The current draft of the new *Joint Technical Standards
for Educational and Psychological Testing* recognizes that educational and psychological testing represents one of the most
important contributions of behavioral science to our society. It
recognizes that testing has provided fundamental and significant
improvements over previous practices in industry, government,
and education and that it has served American society well in
providing a tool for broader and more equitable access to education and employment. While not all tests are well developed and

not all testing practices are wise and beneficial, available evidence clearly supports the judgment of the Committee on Ability Testing of the National Academy of Sciences that the proper use of well-constructed and validated tests provides a far better basis for making decisions about individuals and programs than would otherwise be available.

Educational and psychological testing has also been the target of extensive scrutiny, criticism, and debate both outside and within the professional testing community. The most frequent criticisms are that tests play too great a role in the lives of students and employees and that tests are biased and exclusionary.

Recent controversies over testing place a heavy burden on the *Standards*. Many issues need to be addressed in a way that does not preempt the political process. In general, the draft *Standards* require that, within feasible limits, the necessary technical information be made available so that those involved in policy debate may be fully informed. The *Standards* do not attempt to provide psychometric answers to policy questions. However, a complete separation of scientific and social concerns is not possible. The requirement in these *Standards* for documentation and scientific analysis may sometimes, in itself, place a substantially greater burden on one side of a policy issue than on another.

Test standards serve three important functions. First, they provide the test developer and test user with guidelines for their own professional work. Most people working in testing are professionals dedicated to doing the best they can with the resources available to them. Standards help them with the difficult decisions of resource allocation. Standards also provide for the informed selection of tests and testing programs by test users.

Second, they tell us what we should and should not expect from tests and test use so that we have a yardstick or standard against which tests and test practices can be evaluated by the professional community. This function is especially important given the well-documented existence of test abuse.

Finally, although the *Standards* are mainly a professional

document guiding practices of members of the three sponsoring organizations, it must be recognized that the *Standards* have been, are, and will be used by the courts in consideration of cases alleging malpractice or improper treatment. The *Standards* also have been, are and will be used in cases involving discrimination or adverse impact in employment selection.

The pursuit of goals of equal opportunity and affirmative action in employment selection by federal agencies and others has led to a high level of litigation during the past 15 years, making those in the testing profession conscious of their vulnerability. Once in the adversarial arena of litigation, people may subordinate common understandings among professionals to considerations of winning a particular case. Statements made in the *Standards* are sometimes quoted out of context or given interpretations by either or both litigants that would not represent professional consensus. The tension of this adversarial context has resulted in an intensified focus on possible misreadings of individual standards by those who have reviewed preliminary drafts of our document. One can only applaud the critical nature of these reviews and acknowledge that the situation makes the development of the new *Standards* a far more difficult process than that faced by any of the previous committees.

Recognizing the importance of external uses of the *Standards,* it has been necessary to make some substantial changes in the new document. Perhaps the most important of these is the labeling of standards as primary, secondary, and conditional rather than essential, very desirable, and desirable. In the 1974 *Standards,* there was a statement to the effect that tests were not expected to literally satisfy all of the essential standards, but rather they were to be judged by whether or not they satisfied the spirit of the document. Such a statement was adequate for internal professional purposes at that time. Given the current intense level of litigation, the new terminology seems to be more appropriate.

In the current, preliminary fourth draft, our definitions are as follows:

The *primary* standards are those that should ideally be met by all tests before their operational use and in all test uses, unless a sound professional reason is available to show why it is not necessary or technically feasible to do so in a particular case.

The *secondary* standards are desirable as goals, but are likely to be beyond reasonable expectation in many situations. While careful consideration of these standards will often be helpful in evaluating tests and programs and in comparing the usefulness of competing instruments, limitations on resources may make adherence to them infeasible in many situations. Test developers and users are not expected to be able to explain why secondary standards, unlike primary standards, have not been met. Secondary standards play two roles: they provide leadership in moving the field to a higher level of professionalism, and they make it easier to compare tests, programs, and uses when a choice among them is possible.

The importance of some standards for test instrumentation will vary with application. These standards are given a *conditional* designation. Such standards should be considered primary for some situations and secondary for others. In deciding whether to take an individual conditional standard as primary or secondary, one must consider carefully its feasibility in relation to the potential consequences to all parties involved in the testing process. Observance of some conditional standards may be difficult for technical or financial reasons for some testing programs, especially those with low volume. However, if the use of the test is likely to have serious consequences for test takers, and especially if a large number of persons are potentially affected, the conditional standards assume increased importance. Finally, it should be noted that the draft *Standards* indicate that any evaluation of a test or testing practice must also take into account a comparison with alternative procedures that might be used.

The placement of standards into categories must be viewed as imperfect. Where testing has a limited role in a larger assessment procedure, for example, in clinical, industrial, or school psychology, some primary standards, especially those dealing with documentation, should be considered as having a secondary designation.

The *Standards* do not require test developers or users to use the document as a checklist or to provide written explanation as to why they did not satisfy particular primary standards. However, they do require developers to caution users on limitations resulting from incomplete research, where a particular use of a test may not yet have been validated.

While there is no time in this brief presentation to chronicle all of the debates that have occurred within the context of the development of test standards, I would like to discuss a few issues that best illustrate the problems our committee has faced.

To the casual observer, it might seem that the profession would surely have a clear and codifiable idea of what it is to say that a test is valid. In fact, the validation of a test is a complex activity and may, depending upon circumstances, be accomplished in a variety of ways. Three different categories of evidence of validity have long been recognized: content-related, criterion-related, and construct-related. The question of what kind of evidence is necessary in a particular situation, what level of evidence is required, and whether evidence from more than one category is necessary is not dictated by the draft *Standards*. Only relatively broad guidelines have been specified. The *Standards* emphasize that great reliance must be placed on the professional judgment of those who produce, use, or review a test. The *Standards* also emphasize that the level of evidence required depends on the role the test will play in a particular application and the extent to which it will have important and lasting effects on test takers. Thus the *Standards* differentiate between measurement and decision uses of a test. The fundamental question is always, "Validity for what?" The general answer to that question involves the clear explication of the role that testing plays in the selection, classification, counseling, certifying, or diagnostic process.

With respect to the charge to the committee, two issues might usefully be discussed. The committee interpreted the requirement that the *Standards* "reflect the current level of consensus of recognized experts" as applying to both substantive and methodological issues. After several attempts to write broad consensus statements, most of what was written was abandoned, much to the chagrin of those who agreed with our statements. Our attempts and our failure verify that a broad consensus is still evolving on such substantive issues as racial and gender differentiated prediction and on such methodological issues as validity generalization and decision theory.

Taken together, two statements in the charge to the committee demand that the *Standards* be precise, concise, and understandable to people with widely varying training and experience. We now have in hand a document that has substantially fewer standards than the 1974 document, but, of necessity, is much longer than 10 commandments.

One of the objectives of the *Standards* revision process is to reduce the probability of test standards being written by the Congress, by the several interested federal agencies, individually by the 50 state legislatures, or individually by the judiciary. My own review of such efforts suggests that they have created as many problems as they have solved. However, if our goal is to be achieved, it is essential that the *Standards* embody a strong ethical imperative, as mentioned in our charge. If the *Standards* are seen as a document serving only the trade interests of the profession, then other groups will provide documents to fill the vacuum. However, if the *Standards* are seen as reflecting the strong concern for the public welfare embodied in other documents of the three sponsoring organizations, then perhaps we can keep the professional process of review of testing practices largely where it is best addressed—within the profession. It is very gratifying to our committee that the excellent review provided by the ad hoc committee of the APA Council of Representatives has given support to our position on this issue. We are hopeful that the fourth draft of the new *Joint Technical Standards for Educational and Psychological Testing* will receive support from the governance of the three sponsoring organizations.*

---

*Both the AERA and NCME subsequently endorsed the fourth draft of the *Joint Technical Standards for Educational and Psychological Testing*. The APA review of the *Standards* had not taken place when this book went to press.

3

Commentaries on the Development
of Technical Standards
for Educational
and Psychological Testing

Anne Anastasi, Frank W. Snyder,
Mary L. Tenopyr, Melvin R. Novick

COMMENTS: ANNE ANASTASI

To begin with, I want to compliment Dr. Novick and the other members of his committee for their courage in undertaking what I originally regarded as an impossible task. To some extent, the initial, impossible dream was already embedded in the nine guidelines formulated by the review committee, which defined the charge to the present implementing committee. But general guidelines can be variously interpreted, and the initial interpretation by the implementing committee rendered its own task even more staggering.

Unquestionably, each draft of the *Standards* reflected sophisticated expertise in psychometrics, together with sensitivity to the societal implications of testing and of performance evaluation in general. The committee was highly qualified for the project and performed a monumental task. Nevertheless, the

Standards set out to attain a truly impossible goal, namely, to provide a single set of detailed specifications fully applicable to the highly diversified population of test developers and test users. Can we realistically undertake to write specific procedural standards that are equally relevant to an independently practicing clinical psychologist with a state licence and a diploma from the American Board of Professional Psychology, to a university professor who is developing an innovative test, and to a school teacher who may or may not have had a course in testing? The first needs high-level qualifications in specialized training and experience, the second needs sophisticated technical information and lofty inspiration, and the third needs readily accessible supervisory and consulting facilities.

The *Standards* were not only designed by a committee, they were also subjected to a flood of inputs from a vast assemblage of advisers, correspondents, and critics, as well as other committees that reviewed one or more drafts. The resulting horse was bound to look like a three-humped camel, with additional sine-wave embellishments.

Against this background, it is gratifying to see signs of a redefinition and clarification of the task, indicating that the committee is now advancing toward a more nearly attainable goal. As Dr. Novick suggested in his paper, the committee has been—and still is—faced with several dilemmas. Let me identify three that I perceived in the concerns expressed by reviewers of the various drafts. These three are the dilemmas: (1) between detailed procedural rules and professional judgment, (2) between ideal test-construction goals and minimum practical standards of test usage, and (3) between technical standards and ethical principles.

I find Dr. Novick's paper especially encouraging as a report of progress toward the resolution of these dilemmas. It reveals a movement away from detailed prescriptions and toward stronger recognition of the role of the properly qualified professional. We cannot evaluate either a test or a particular use of that test without also evaluating the test user. Let us not forget that a psychological test is a tool, like a surgeon's scalpel. In their own way, psychological tests can be just as beneficial when properly used—and just as deadly if improperly used. The qualifications of the test user will remain a primary factor in proper test usage. The test user serves a major and decisive function at two stages: first, in the evaluation and selection of a test for a specific purpose; second, in the interpretation and application of test scores actually obtained by individuals. Test users need at least an elementary knowledge of test-construction procedures in order to assess the data provided in the technical manual and, on this basis, to choose the appropriate test and interpret its scores correctly. Both stages require also professional training and expertise in the content area in which the test is used, as illustrated by educational, clinical, or industrial settings. And across all settings, proper test use requires some current knowledge of behavioral science, especially as it pertains to the origins and etiology of human behavior and the limits of modifiability of the behaviors assessed by test scores. The test user who cannot personally meet these qualifications needs to be in touch with a supervisor or a consultant who has the necessary expertise.

With regard to the second dilemma, that between ideal goals and professionally acceptable standards, a possible resolution was suggested by the ad hoc committee of the APA Council of Representatives that reviewed the third draft of the *Standards* (see *Report . . .* , 1983, Recommendation No. 1). The recommendation was that the *Standards* be separated into two parts: one part to provide technical standards for test development, the other to provide principles of test usage. Part I would include not only technical standards but also technical goals— ideal procedures that are beyond the current state of the art; it would thus encourage continuing technical progress and innovation. Part II, on principles of test usage, would permit verification of conformity to realistic and acceptable professional practice. Admittedly, this is only one proposed solution. There may be others that fit the situation better. But the underlying dilemma is important and should be taken into account.

The third dilemma, between technical standards and ethical principles, is discussed in Dr. Novick's paper, which refers to the original charge to the committee that the *Standards* should "embody a strong ethical imperative." Dr. Novick expresses gratification that the ad hoc committee of the APA Council had given strong support to his committee's position on this issue. It is well to note exactly what the APA committee recommended in this regard. The statement reads:

> Many of the comments object to Draft 3's "mixing of ethics with principles and standards." However, the ad hoc Committee recognizes the need in certain instances to articulate standards or principles that have implications for professional ethics. In such instances, the ad hoc Committee recommends that reference be made to specific standards in the *APA Ethical Principles of Psychologists*. (Report . . . , 1983, Recommendation No. 7)

The ad hoc committee does *not* recommend interspersing ethical principles, such as those pertaining to confidentiality and informed consent, among the technical standards. Besides engendering confusion, such a treatment would necessarily provide inadequate and incomplete coverage of the applicable principles of professional ethics; the latter can be handled more clearly, fully, and appropriately in a separate document.

Finally, let me refer to a more specific substantive matter. I am pleased to see that the treatment of validation procedures is being broadened and made more flexible than was the case in the earlier drafts. It is also encouraging to learn that the term "components of validity" is being replaced by "categories of evidence." The connotations of these two terms, in both theory and practice, are quite different. In the earlier drafts, the treatment of validation in general—and more particularly, of construct validation—was open to considerable misunderstanding and confusion. If rigidly applied, in a checklist fashion, it could have led to incorrect decisions in both test construction and test usage. Many critics of earlier drafts were seriously concerned about these undesirable albeit unintended consequences. In fact, the situation seems to have brought on an epidemic of a new form of anxiety in our culture. We are all familiar with test anxiety. Recently there has appeared a syndrome that can be best described as test-standards anxiety. The progress revealed in today's report of the work of the *Joint Technical Standards* committee should go far toward reducing the prevalence of this syndrome.

Reference

Report of the First Meeting of the Ad Hoc Committee of the Council of Representatives to Review the Draft Joint Technical Standards, June 11-12, 1983. American Psychological Association, Council of Representatives, Agenda Item No. 121, Supplemental Enclosure, August 1983.

COMMENTS: FRANK W. SNYDER

I appreciate this opportunity to respond publicly to the *Standards*. CTB/McGraw-Hill has spent considerable time reviewing the prior two drafts of the *Standards* and looks forward to continuing that effort on the fourth draft. Although I find it ironic that neither a representative of the publishers, who are to develop tests in conformity with the *Standards,* nor representatives of the test users, who ultimately will put the *Standards to* their "test," were included as members of the committee, I have made every effort to weigh my reactions both as a psychometrician and as a publisher. Given the direction that revisions to the *Standards* have taken toward more user responsibility, every effort should be made to include both developers and users in subsequent revision efforts.

The committee is to be sincerely congratulated for its fine accomplishment in examining a most complex social issue and bringing together recommendations for the *Standards*. Reducing to written form such a diverse range of testing philosophies is in itself a monumental task. The committee should be highly commended for its positive reactions to the reviews of the preliminary drafts and for its skill in dealing with the criticisms received.

I have found the task of summarizing CTB's overall reactions to the *Standards* a difficult one. I find myself caught in a dilemma. On the one hand, I want to applaud the efforts of the committee. The magnitude of the task undertaken was enormous, and the quantity and quality of the results are clearly substantial. On the other hand, I would abrogate my responsibilities if I did not point out that there have been and still are some points of philosophical and practical disagreement with the directions taken by the *Standards* committee.

It is my strong belief that the *Standards* should be just that. Once agreed on, the *Standards* will become the goals that test technicians and users should strive to attain. Standards, then, should represent clearly specified goals. Those standards that have not been agreed on by a consensus of the profession should be omitted until agreement emerges. The nature of standards themselves should not be ignored. They should not pre-scribe specific processes, procedures, or data to be collected or reported, but confine themselves to the goals a test should satisfy.

Given the changing environment in testing and technol-ogy, I believe it is nonproductive, perhaps even counterpro-ductive, to include the processes by which the *Standards* are to be met. Such elaborate prescriptions of the processes that test construction and supporting data should follow will, in the long run, tend to stifle new, creative approaches to psycho-metric techniques.

I believe the committee properly acknowledged the im-plications of such consequences when dealing with standards that "reflect the current lack of consensus of recognized ex-perts" by stating that "a broad consensus is still evolving" on such substantial issues as racial and gender-differentiated pre-diction and on such methodological issues as validity generali-zation and decision theory. A difficult decision it must have been, particularly in view of the comprehensive effort that was displayed, and I commend the committee's decision and its openness.

Although the current draft of the *Standards* contains some forty fewer standards than the 1974 edition, and a reduc-tion of some sixty from the prior draft, I am left with the over-all impression that there are too many, demanding too much detail. The committee should pay careful attention to the elab-orate detail required by some standards. While we may concur with the *Standards* in principle, it is absurd to ignore the practi-cal realities of limited research and development budgets. If documentation is required to fulfill an arbitrary requirement of independent replicability, we may substantially decrease the number of innovative efforts within existing types of tests and curtail the development of new ones.

I do not feel that the committee has dealt adequately with the issue of the number and classification of standards. In addition to considering the number of primary standards too large and requiring too much detail, I am also concerned about the classification method itself. The distinction between secondary and conditional standards is not clear and could lead to the very type of legal haggling the *Standards* attempt to avoid. If it is not possible to specify a small set of broad desiderata to which tests should conform, then I would suggest that demands for specific data and/or procedures are finding their way into individual standards. This is to be avoided if consensus is to be reached.

One final specific point: I believe references are badly needed. If there are reasons not to include them in the *Standards* themselves, then an adjunct publication should be developed. This should first provide a general set of annotated references designed to guide professionals who are not psychometricians but who are engaged in either test use or test construction. Second, a list of specific technical references should be made available that gives details about how one might proceed to achieve the goals of the various specific standards. These should be cross-referenced to the *Standards*.

Despite my comments, I still agree wholeheartedly with the committee that standards must be developed by the psychometric community, not the legislature or the judiciary. Those of us who have had to testify before legislative or judicial bodies know the frustration of attempting to explain the various dimensions of testing theory and applied statistics. Also, I concur that the final *Standards* must embody the strong ethical imperative that Melvin Novick so aptly states, for we must be serving societal interests, not our own.

This brings me to my last point and one that I feel should be of deep concern to all of us committed to the proper use of tests and test results. Novick alludes to it in reference to the national goals of equal opportunity and affirmative action, but in my opinion the threat of litigation is much wider and covers the construction, supporting documentation, and use of test results at all levels.

Until this time professional standards have not had the force of law. That may soon change. In February 1983, the California Assembly passed a bill (AB-621, Klehs) related to employment testing and intrusion into employees' personal lives. The existing *Standards* were specifically cited in the bill, stating in effect that tests that were in compliance with the *Standards* would be exempt from the provisions of the bill:

> This subdivision shall not apply to any stan-
> dardized psychological test or examination in com-
> pliance with the provisions of the American Psy-
> chological Association "Standards for Educational
> and Psychological Tests (1974)."

Although the bill was defeated in the Senate, it has been put up for reconsideration in the 1984 session. If the bill is passed, the *Standards* will become a statutory obligation.

I believe the committee senses its own vulnerability in setting standards. The fact that it requested an opinion from counsel (Ennis and others, 1983) relating to the committee's liability supports this belief. The opinion states that "there is very little likelihood that the *Standards* will place any of the three sponsoring organizations or their members in legal jeopardy." However, this assurance does not carry over to test developers and users. The opinion goes on to cite our vulnerability in proving that we have exercised the necessary "standard of care" required to absolve us of professional misconduct. "Standard of care" is an elusive and subjective yardstick. It is greatly influenced by the persuasive talents of the plaintiff in demonstrating that due care in meeting the standard of care in the case at hand had not been exercised. Quoting further from the opinion:

> It is possible, therefore, that the *Standards*
> could be introduced as persuasive evidence estab-
> lishing the standard of care for evaluating the prac-
> tices of particular publishers, developers, and prac-
> titioners, even though the *Standards* themselves
> claim only a modest role in such adjudication.

Although it is true that the *Standards* are described only as a basis for evaluating the quality of all testing practices and thus permit defendants to rebut with evidence that they did in fact comply, this places a stronger onus on the writers of the new *Standards* to refrain from setting forth detailed procedures that may be impossible to follow. The *Standards* should set goals; they should not attempt to control processes.

I strongly urge that before the *Standards* are published in final form, they be subjected first to extensive legal review for opinions on the effect they will have should they become a part of the definitional process in new legislation.

I urge the committee to consider the far-reaching implications of the *Standards*, which will surely be our industry's most important and vital document. If they are constrained by detailed prescriptions, the entire psychometric community is placed in a defensive position. Let us keep the *Standards* concise. Let us publish those on which there is consensus and leave the others for later amendments. Let us realize the need for practicality when the *Standards* are translated into applications. Let us adopt standards that will epitomize the best goals of our profession and not restrain experimentation and innovation. And finally, let us find a way to broaden the standard-setting process to include those in our profession not working in an academic environment and the users whose use or misuse of tests will ultimately determine their impact on society.

Reference

B. Ennis, P. Friedman, D. Bersoff, and M. Ewing. *Legal Review of Joint Technical Standards for Educational and Psychological Testing.* January 5, 1983.

COMMENTS: MARY L. TENOPYR

Going beyond the exact provisions of the *Joint Technical Standards for Educational and Psychological Testing,* I want to address the many questions of the role of standards in a professional organization. The *Joint Technical Standards* merely provide exemplary material for this discussion. If I may summarize what Dr. Novick has said, I see three goals for standards: (1) improving practice, (2) preventing harm, and (3) serving political purposes, such as prevention of regulation by outside entities. I shall discuss each of these goals in turn and then offer some suggestions of my own. First, whether or not the goal of improving practice is achieved depends on more than the content of the standards. Testing, for example, as every other professional practice, exists as part of large systems. We must consider all parts of the systems and their interrelationships to determine the effects of standards on practice.

We must particularly recognize that these are not necessarily rational systems and that standards presumably conceived in rationality may not have rational effects. For example, we as testing professionals sometimes act as if we believe that measurement is well accepted in the world. We know that sound measurement is beneficial, yet does the rest of the world know it? I contend that much of society essentially equates testing with reading Tarot cards or examining the entrails of birds. Professional standards are often supported by analogies to standards for housing or automobiles. I believe that testing standards are more like standards for avocados, a fruit not well known to a large segment of the population and often called by the unflattering name of alligator pear, which has many unpleasant connotations. If detailed and, to a large extent, unachievable standards were set up for producers and eaters of avocados, the result would be simple. A nonessential food like avocados would not be eaten and, hence, not produced.

People, in general, cannot do without housing or transportation, but they can do without avocados. When it becomes too difficult to eat avocados, it does avocado supporters little good to make arguments, such as that the fruit has more nutritive

value than some alternate fruit to which such essentially unachievable standards are not applied. As could happen with the
avocado, testing, as we have seen, has practically been eliminated by overly stringent regulation in the private employment
area.

Psychological measurement is not fully developed or accepted in the world. However irrational we think the beliefs
about testing may be, we must contend with them. We must
recognize that well-meaning but ill-conceived standards may
threaten the very existence of testing. We must also consider
that in a rational world all professional work would be controlled by professionals. This, as we all know, is not the case.
The control of resources, both human and economic, to support good measurement is in the hands of others than measurement experts. Furthermore, most of the actual decisions that
affect the lives of people in education and occupations are not
made by measurement specialists. Standards by professional organizations to which the decision makers do not belong can be
expected to have little impact. The fact that these people, for
the most part, cannot understand the standards, but are an
important part of the systems in which measurement exists,
must be recognized.

Standards will improve practice only to the degree to
which an infrastructure that will support the standards is in
place. A business would not set up new standards for its prod-
ucts in a vacuum. Many parts of the total business system would
be examined and provisions made for altering or strengthening
those parts that would hinder achieving the standards. For
example, equipment might have to be upgraded, new plants
built, workers trained, or new inspection systems put into place.

Psychological standards too, cannot be established as a
single self-contained effort. The standards will be ineffective as
long as the system to support the standards is not there. In the
majority of universities in this country, one cannot even take a
series of advanced courses in psychometrics. Furthermore, in
many psychology departments, one cannot find a simple course
in testing. In my discussions with a number of people in aca-
demia, I have found that many department heads fail to recog-

nize even the basic needs for psychometric education. In part, this is the result of a vicious cycle. If the employers of educational and industrial psychologists do not either understand the need for psychometric education or fail to demand it, the schools will fail to offer it. In business, where testing has for all practical purposes been eliminated by government regulation, the law of supply and demand essentially seems to have taken effect. With testing curtailed, there is no need for persons educated in measurement, and hence, measurement is not taught.

If we want to improve testing practices, we must build the educational infrastructure for educators, students, and employers so that the value of sound measurement is recognized and delivery systems are put in place to provide the education needed to understand and comply with any measurement standards produced. The psychometricians must broaden their sphere of communication so that education in psychometrics is not limited to an elite few.

The second goal of standards, to prevent harm, leads to some complex issues. First there is the question: What is the greatest harm? Second there is the question: Who is being harmed? These two questions lead to a host of issues involving value systems. For example, using an employment test with only marginal validity may harm a number of individuals who are rejected for jobs yet result in enough productivity gains for the employer to keep him or her from bankruptcy and thereby enable the continuance of a number of jobs in the community. This is not to recommend using tests of marginal validity, but it is one example of the ambiguity and possible controversy that surrounds the concept of doing harm and that indicates how value systems can affect one's perception of harm.

There is another consideration. If test standards become so unachievable that testing is abandoned, is there more or less harm done? If employers and educators move away from testing to the unvalidated alternatives like unstructured interviews conducted by nonprofessionals, I contend that there is potentially more harm done to a greater number of persons. Again, it must be remembered that testing does not exist within a necessarily rational system and that the education base for those who make the crucial decisions about what assessment procedures to use is weak.

Many have pointed to the unsatisfactory testing practices that, it cannot be denied, exist in this country. There is no question that there are some fringe operators in test development and use, but their existence is not a justification for new standards. It appears that many of these problematic practices represent a deliberate flaunting of the standards that have existed in the profession since 1954. Certainly, no new standards can be expected to have any effect on these operations. Again, what are needed are educational programs for those who buy these services so that the sources of income for the fringe operators are eliminated.

The standards' third goal, to prevent outside regulation, is in theory a desirable end. However, whether that end will be satisfactorily achieved is dependent on a number of factors. It must be understood that government regulation of testing has political and social aims. The forces that promote such regulation appear to want the most stringent standards that can be achieved for testing regardless of any other considerations. Earlier drafts of the *Joint Technical Standards* were more stringent than any regulation of testing that now exists. Few court decisions have imposed any requirements more stringent than those of earlier versions of the *Standards*. Certainly, those who oppose testing should welcome the *Standards* and be eager to incorporate them in regulations or use them in court.

The very fact that professional organizations issue standards implies that these standards can be met in the vast majority of cases. It also implies that there is an infrastructure and common consensus built up to support these standards. This certainly is not the case with the *Standards*. Their incorporation into law could have a negative effect on the image of the educational and psychological measurement organizations. Again, we cannot produce standards in a vacuum and must build up the infrastructure first before we develop stringent standards that may become law. It is naive to believe that the resources, both human and financial, needed to support sound testing will flow from the imposition of overly strict testing standards and their incorporation into law.

In summary, it should be reiterated that testing is part of many systems, many of which do not necessarily operate by the rational rules of science to which we are accustomed. If we wish to preserve testing and improve it, we must work toward changing the systems. Organizations cannot appoint an ad hoc committee to devise standards and then walk away, having officially done the job. We need total support from the educational and psychological organizations to formulate a planned approach to improving psychometrics in this country. Those whose psychometric education is beyond that of the average educator or psychologist have a special obligation to work within these organizations to help those whose educational background limits their comprehension of psychometrics. It is far easier to condemn those not fortunate enough to be well educated in psychometrics than to help them. Furthermore, we must educate the consumers of psychometrics so that they provide the organizational and financial support necessary for proper measurement and eschew the purveyors of unsound testing.

In the meantime, any standards on testing should be in the form of general principles and be presented for guidance of the professional, not for adoption by the courts. These principles should not freeze practice in its current state, but should represent achievable goals and be the basis for broad programs to improve measurement. The detailed psychometric prescriptions should be left for the educational materials that are so badly needed.

I personally pledge to do my part in the effort to build up the educational and organizational infrastructure that is the necessary underpinning of refined standards. I hope to see the day within a decade when the educational and psychological organizations can issue meaningful detailed standards and say in truth that their members can comply with these standards.

A RESPONSE TO CRITICISMS OF THE DRAFT
JOINT TECHNICAL STANDARDS: MELVIN R. NOVICK

I want to thank ETS for this opportunity to present our case for the adoption of the new test standards, for providing three articulate critics as discussants, and for providing me the opportunity to respond in some detail. The quality of the discussion has been very high, as would be expected from the three distinguished discussants. Their criticism has touched on important and sensitive issues and will require careful response. In making my response, I shall refer to these three papers and to some other comments that have been received on our preliminary fourth draft.

There is a long history of joint test standards development by the AERA, APA, and NCME. The present committee effort has been observant of that tradition except where divergence seemed necessary. Some of our critics, however, imply that we depart from that tradition. I do not believe that they are correct. First, with regard to the composition of the committee, I note that the *Standards* have never been prepared by a committee representing special interests, such as test publishers. They have always been prepared by measurement specialists who were primarily university based, but known for their expertise in testing applications. If the Joint Test Standards revision committee were composed of representatives of special interests, it would be an unwieldy committee. We would need several test publishers to cover the field, an elementary school teacher, a high school teacher, a university professor, a college admissions officer, a guidance counselor, an occupational licensor, and a minimum of 30 other persons.

Note also that there are at least two dozen professional organizations with interests in testing. Instead of seeking representation from all of these organizations, the three sponsors, consistent with tradition, opted for technical rather than political coverage. However, to ensure that all voices were heard, over 100 advisers were appointed, and the third draft was, and the fourth draft will be, made available to all association members who wish to review it. At least one person employed by each major publisher served as an adviser to our committee.

Some of the critics have called for the reduction of the test standards to 10 commandments, others to a document the size of the Bill of Rights, and others to a document of a page or two saying that validity is the most important aspect of test justification and "adding an embellishment or two." On the other hand, there are those who have insisted that every standard in the 1974 document is sacred and should be included in the new document. They would also add many new requirements. I believe that the proposals of both sets of critics are inconsistent with tradition. Our committee, with the essential help provided by our advisers, has been struggling to provide a document with adequate coverage, brevity, and precision. We have discarded many standards from the 1974 document that addressed policy rather than technical issues, and we have refined, generalized, or combined others. Despite the fact that our current working draft—which only the committee itself and selected advisers, including the three discussants, have seen—is shorter by 45 standards than the 1974 document, each of the three discussants recommends further radical surgery. I don't believe this can be done and still maintain a meaningful document. I am pleased, however, that none of the discussants alleged, in their presentations, that the draft *Standards* are a political document.

With regard to length, I note that many of the most severe critics of the present document have also been very vocal in insisting on a standard or standards to reflect their own particular interests. One states that "the *Standards* draft appears to have ignored all considerations of copyright and trade protection." I note, however, that there is a specific standard on test security, copyright, and trade secrets. We could elaborate this into three or four standards giving detailed requirements. But to do this in even a few areas would greatly increase the length of the document. Another critic argues that many of our standards are good but require a slightly different statement in a variety of different areas. This critic simultaneously argues that our current draft is too long.

Dr. Snyder strongly supports our position on ethical standards. Dr. Anastasi admonishes us not to mix ethical and technical standards. She does this despite clear precedent. I quote, in brief, from my letter of June 8, 1983, to the ad hoc committee of the APA Council of Representatives in which I argued for their inclusion. "First, we note that these are the kinds of standards by which all researchers must live. . . . in research there is danger of negative impact [but] it is remote. . . . In practical applications the danger is less remote." Next, I would point out that there is precedent in the 1974 *Standards* for standards that are largely ethical in nature. I refer to standard J2.1, which is not only an ethical standard, as a matter of judgment, but one that is specifically identified as such. Next, I would point to a letter from Nancy Cole, writing in her capacity as president of the National Council on Measurement in Education, reflecting the views of the NCME Executive Committee strongly supporting the inclusion of ethical standards. I refer also to the letter from T. Anne Cleary, vice president of AERA, representing the Measurement and Research Methodology Division, which takes a similar stand.

Turning again to the statement of the committee of the APA Council, I quote: "Many of the comments object to Draft 3's 'mixing of ethics with principles and standards.' However, the ad hoc Committee recognizes the need in certain instances for standards or principles that have implications for professional ethics. . . ."

Dr. Anastasi follows this quote with her own *interpretation* that the ad hoc committee does *not* recommend interspersing ethical principles, such as those pertaining to confidentiality and informed consent, among the technical standards. On the basis of the arguments I presented to the APA committee and their *stated* position, I conclude that the dictum offered by Dr. Anastasi involves a distinct break with tradition and is inconsistent with the desires of all test publishers and consumer advocates with whom we have corresponded. The standard dealing with test security, copyright, and trade secrets is an ethical standard that belongs in our document. This standard protects test developers and is essential, as are those involving test confidentiality and informed consent that protect test takers.

Dr. Anastasi's suggestion that ethical issues can be "handled more clearly, fully, and appropriately in a separate document" leaves me confused. Are we to convene a second Joint Technical Standards committee to prepare standards for the ethical use of tests? Or does Dr. Anastasi suggest that this should be done by a standing APA committee? In the latter case, it would appear that Dr. Anastasi is suggesting that one of the most important aspects of testing be treated by a single organization rather than be a joint effort of AERA, APA, and NCME. Such a practice would be a sharp break from tradition and would and should, in my judgment, jeopardize the public acceptance of the *Standards*.

Despite the apparent sharp disagreement on this issue, it is possible that a compromise can be fashioned. Following the conference, Dr. Anastasi and I discussed the possibility of "gathering up" into a separate section many of the standards that deal largely with ethical matters. Such a section might be called "Administrative Procedures." This would have the benefit of a reduction in intermingling but still keep the treatment of ethical issues in testing within the single standards document. I might add that following the conference I received a letter from the APA Board of Social and Ethical Responsibility very strongly supporting the inclusion of ethical issues in the *Standards*.

Dr. Anastasi suggests that our committee faces three major dilemmas. I have responded to her third. I now turn to the first, the suggested conflict between detailed procedural rules and professional judgment. Dr. Snyder and Dr. Tenopyr join Dr. Anastasi in taking a firm stand against detailed procedural rules, but I believe that we have come closer in the preliminary fourth draft to resolving this dilemma.

The dilemma between detailed procedural rules and professional judgment arises because, on the one hand, vaguely specified generalized goals provide a very poor basis for evaluating a test or testing practice, while, on the other hand, specific requirements provide insufficient latitude for the use of viable and possibly preferable alternatives to standard practice in some situations. Particularly disturbing to the discussants is the statement of specific reporting requirements. This is a dilemma for which there is no solution that will be satisfactory to all parties in the test process. The present draft of the *Standards,* however, adopts what I believe to be a very reasonable compromise. It does suggest certain specific reporting requirements at various points in the document but precedes this with the clear statement that the test developer or user always has the option of satisfying any standard by alternative means and that no specific requirement of any standard is absolute. This approach was taken in the 1974 document but was stated with insufficient forcefulness and was undercut by the label "essential." Again, I reiterate the point made in my paper. Lack of specification in the *Standards* invites the imposition of such specificity by those untrained in psychometric methods or having their own political agenda.

Dr. Anastasi's second dilemma, that between ideal goals and professionally acceptable standards, drew the suggestion by the APA ad hoc committee that the *Standards* be separated into two parts, one part to provide technical standards for test development and the other to provide principles of test usage. The recommendation was also made that our committee enlist the support of specialists in the various areas of test use so that topics in the various areas could be treated at a level of detail comparable to that found, for example, in the Division 14 *Principles for Employment Testing.* The response of the Joint Technical Standards committee to this suggestion was not positive for a variety of reasons.

First, the division into two documents seems counterproductive. The first two chapters of the draft *Standards* contain material on validity and reliability that is basic to both test development and test use. It would therefore be necessary to have comparable versions of these two chapters in both volumes. To a somewhat lesser extent, the same argument could be made concerning material contained in all chapters of Part I, which provides standards that test users must have to evaluate tests they are considering for adoption. Similarly, Part II on test use must be studied by test developers so that they may know what information the test users need in order to do their work properly. Second, the adoption of the APA committee's recommendation concerning level of detail would result in a second volume of enormous size. The level of detail in the Division 14 *Principles* is far greater than should be contained in the *Standards,* and this is only one of perhaps six areas that require coverage. Finally, the distinction between test developer and test user is an idealized distinction. Many testers, including Dr. Tenopyr, are both developers and users.

Our solution to this dilemma has been to combine and generalize standards on test use when this is possible and to provide brief treatments in six specialized areas of application. This approach carries with it the recommendation that derivative documents, comparable to the Division 14 *Principles,* be prepared in each of the six areas. Such documents now exist in most of these areas. Some of these have been prepared by organizations not involved in the development of the *Standards.* Having divided the field of testing into six, admittedly arbitrary, parts, the specialty standards in each area could be addressed by a team of experts in each field having more depth than is present in our committee. In preparing these derivative documents, the specialty area committees should be bound only to respect the primacy of the *Standards,* but in every other way should have freedom to develop their own standards or principles. The only essential requirement would be consistency with the *Standards.* I emphasize that what I propose is a very traditional and proven solution to a problem that is not new. The proposal here only sharpens the relationship between the primary and the derivative documents. It may be worth suggesting that these derivative documents have traditionally provided the references to the literature that Dr. Snyder desires. The *Standards* themselves have never provided references for several excellent reasons.

Dr. Snyder has raised a point that requires careful response. He states: "If documentation is required to fulfill an arbitrary requirement of independent replicability, we may substantially decrease the number of innovative efforts." In fact, the *Standards* do not discourage innovation. Instead the *Standards* carefully specify in the introduction that tests may be introduced with only partial validation, provided it can be argued that the test is preferable to the clearly visible alternatives, that announcements clearly indicate the limitations of the research base, that necessary cautions are given, and that research continues. The critical point here is that no greater claim should be made for a test than is warranted by its research base.

Dr. Snyder's final point of concern is that "until this time professional standards have not had the force of law [but] that may soon change." He refers to a bill passed by the California Assembly but later defeated in the California Senate. In fact, this is not the first piece of testing legislation at the state level. There is a long history of the *Standards'* having had the force of law. Some time ago, Dr. Bersoff provided me with a long computer-search listing of cases in which the *Standards* were cited as authority in legal proceedings. In response to Dr. Snyder, I can only reaffirm the statement made in my paper that we must write strong and specific standards for ourselves, or others will write them for us. Better to have our *Standards* adopted by reference than to have them written in Sacramento and 49 other state capitals.

I wish now to address Dr. Tenopyr's thesis that we should have less rigorous new standards than we have had in the past because we no longer have enough trained workers to properly conduct testing programs. Instead, she argues, we should accept lower quality work until the necessary infrastructure can be built over the next decade. I do not accept this thesis.

During the past decade, employment testers have been much engaged in litigation. As a result, the training of testing persons in universities and in service has deemphasized the technical aspects of testing and embraced the study of legal issues. Rewards went to those with expertise in administrative and legal procedures rather than to those with expertise in psychometrics. Testing itself was also viewed unenthusiastically by some who do not recognize that testing has historically been one of the foremost instruments of equality of opportunity in this country. On the other hand, many colleges of education now have stronger programs in testing than ever before, and the quality of research and teaching in this area is at a new peak, as is the capacity to train and retrain students.

I concur with Dr. Tenopyr that something should be done to revitalize the teaching of testing in departments of psychology by making available the expertise that resides dormant there. However, Dr. Tenopyr's suggestion that we lower standards is likely to result in the opposite of the desired effect. Lowering the requirement and hence the demand for technical expertise will not raise the supply of technically trained persons. Instead, what is needed is a concerted effort to upgrade the capabilities of those now in the field and to entice new persons into the field. There are traditional and proven ways of doing this, including training sessions, sabbaticals, fellowship programs, and internships. While there are many such programs involving testing and the law, there are only a few involving the technical aspects of testing.

The major testing organizations now do some in-service training. They could easily do more, provided funds were available. The same could be said of some colleges of education and some departments of psychology. The University of Iowa is prepared to accept 20 persons for a two-year master's program in testing each year. Those persevering would be fully qualified to work in all fields of testing application.

Finally, let me respond to Dr. Tenopyr's remark that we "cannot appoint an ad hoc committee to devise standards and then walk away, having officially done the job." It is my intent, and that of every member of the Joint Technical Standards revision committee, to work within the three professional organizations to help "those whose educational background limits their comprehension of psychometrics." It is also my intention to do what I can to ensure that the *Standards,* when adopted, are not used as a club to intimidate those testing professionals whose work is at an acceptable level of professionalism and provides a preferable alternative to no testing at all.

4

Role of Testing
in Developing and Assessing
Early Childhood
Education Programs

Anthony J. Alvarado

The 1983 Invitational Conference gives me an opportunity to share a dilemma we face in the New York City Public Schools and to ask for help in dealing with it. The dilemma affects our recent initiative to guarantee full-day kindergarten to all five-year-olds. As a public school system, we need reliable information on the results of our effort to help these young children learn. At the same time, however, the state of testing technology for children this age is seriously limited, perhaps inherently so.

Goals of Early Childhood Education

With our country's public schools thrust into the national spotlight, this is an opportune time for educators to press for advances in the quality and context of education. The public outcry for reform is sincere, widespread, and well informed. Our constituency knows the magnitude and gravity of the problems that plague the schools. Our students do not read, comprehend, or think nearly as well as we expect them to. Students from other lands consistently outperform our students in math and science. Our corporations and industries tell us that the graduates of our schools have neither the proper skills nor the proper attitudes toward work to be fully productive employees. Forty-five percent of our New York City youth do not even finish high school, and the figure is shockingly higher for minority youth.

We will not abandon the young people who have grown up in our schools or those who have come to us in the later years. But if we care about the future of our nation and our children, we must attend now to the newest entrants into our school system.

In September 1983, the New York City Public Schools implemented the first step of a multiyear early childhood strategy designed to prevent school failure by providing an enriched and challenging all-day kindergarten program. This is one of the first components of my Agenda for Achievement in the New York City Public Schools. Over the next four years, we will move up through the grades, focusing on one grade each year, revamping, enriching, and generally improving our early childhood programs. We will institute new curricula that require more of our students and emphasize comprehension, reasoning, and problem solving. We will add to this a more demanding program of oral communication and writing. This effort will entail paraprofessional support in kindergarten and grade one and continuing professional development to enhance staff capacities in these critical areas.

Our decision to focus on early childhood education as one of our first initiatives was informed by research that is widely known among educators. Studies of children who have participated in Head Start, Follow Through, and similar enrichment programs have shown that these children outperformed nonparticipants on various measures of intellectual functioning and school readiness (Bissell, 1973; Systems Development Corporation, 1972). They were less likely to experience failure or to be retained in later grades (Lazar and Darlington, 1982; Nieman and Gastright, 1981). Research has demonstrated that in terms of academic and social development, all-day kindergarten programs have advantages over half-day programs (McClinton and Topping, 1981; Winter and Klein, 1970).

We expect that, as a result of this new policy, we will see growth in cognition as well as in motor skills, communication, and socialization. We expect that these skills will help our children to make a smoother transition into the first grade. These are our short-term goals.

We have other, more far-reaching goals as well. In my judgment, a decision to improve early childhood education will have a long-range, positive impact on education at all levels. We expect our early childhood program, in combination with efforts at the junior high and high school levels, to reduce greatly our high school dropout rate, now double the national average. We expect to see a reduction in special education referrals—a major problem in New York City.

Program Assessment

The all-day kindergarten is central to our shift of emphasis from remediation to prevention. It is a key element in our response to the public outcry for educational reform. The assessment of early childhood programs, however, is perilous—an educational minefield we must cross only with the utmost attention and care. Assessment is particularly difficult due to the scope of the New York City program, variation in implementation across districts, lack of an appropriate comparison group, and problems with standardized testing in general and with testing of young children in particular.

Scope of the Program. Some 55,000 children are enrolled in all-day kindergartens at 600 elementary schools throughout the city. The size of this population means that we must in some way limit our use of individually administered, time-consuming measurement tools.

Furthermore, assessment of a population of this size and diversity is susceptible to many of the problems inherent in evaluating a broad-scale, national early childhood program. We must make every effort to sidestep the pitfalls documented, for example, in reviews of the assessment of the Follow Through program (House and others, 1978).

Local Variation in Program Services. Although we have distributed all-day kindergarten program guidelines to the thirty-two Community School Districts, the district superintendents make final decisions about program implementation. For this reason, we will be testing children who participate in a variety of instructional programs, with different curricula and emphases.

Lack of Appropriate Comparison Group. Comparison with a control group—a sample of similar students in a similar environment who are not receiving program services—would help us to distinguish program effects from results that might be expected in the absence of the program. But, since virtually all kindergarten children in the city's public schools will be enrolling in all-day kindergarten classes, we will not have an appropriate comparison group. Historical comparison with New York City children is not an option for studying program impact in its first year; because kindergarten students are not included in the annual citywide achievement testing, there is no existing data base from which to construct a comparison group. However, as all-day kindergarten children move through the grades, comparative studies will allow us to discern the long-term impact of our initiative.

Testing Young Children

The most difficult problem we face in assessing the impact of the all-day kindergarten program is measuring student growth in cognition, motor skills, communication, and socialization. The typical yardstick for student performance has been the standardized test. If we are to continue to use these tests in reporting on our efforts, we must be sure that the results will be understood by the public and, at the same time, be meaningful to educators and policy planners. We need tests that are technically sound—that have a high degree of validity and reliability. We need tests that are in no way detrimental to our students. And we need tests that are fair.

These standards present challenges at every grade level. The public and the educational research community have called into question some of the uses to which standardized tests have been put. They have questioned the appropriateness of specific tests for various populations. Some change has occurred—we are moving toward greater reliability in some areas. But in one area—the testing of the youngest children entrusted to us—we do not yet have measurement tools that fully meet our standards. For the characteristics of these young children pose thorny technical problems. And many proposed solutions —such as repeated individualized testing or structured observation over time—would excessively strain our resources.

We face this dilemma: On the one hand, we need to know and report how well we are accomplishing our task of teaching these small children; on the other hand, we do not yet have acceptable standardized tests with which to assess their progress reliably, nor do we have satisfactory ways to distinguish the impact of our program from other influences that promote development and from the natural maturation process. My specific concerns are:

- The effects of testing on young children;
- The effects of testing on children's classroom experience;
- The appropriateness of various tests for children of our city. Do they measure the right things? Enough things? For which populations?; and
- The utility of testing: for parents, for teachers, and for policy planners.

Researchers have described characteristics of young children that require us to proceed with the greatest care when we measure their progress (Haney and Gelberg, 1980). Variability in the rate of maturation in the very young, their short attention span for tasks they have not chosen themselves, and their tendency to interpret questions strictly in light of their own experience pose problems for test givers. For the youngest students, tests usually must be administered individually and orally. Even in this context, variability due to the testing situation, including the ethnicity of the test giver, is greater than with older children.

With young children, we are not testing mastery of a particular curriculum, as we often are with older students. We are measuring more general aspects of development—cognition, motor skills, communication, socialization—that cannot be closely matched to a specific curriculum. Even if we can develop tests that take into account the unique characteristics of young children, it is still difficult to interpret the results—to separate the effects of classroom experience from the influence of the home environment. And norms are often severely limited for this population.

These are some of the difficulties faced by test designers in developing instruments for use with young children, and they have not yet been overcome. Researchers have concluded that early childhood tests are significantly lower in technical quality than those used with older children. They are often poor in terms of validity and reliability (Haney and Gelberg, 1980).

The Effects of Testing on Children. We are concerned about the effects of testing on our young children. We do not want to instill a fear of testing, or a fear of failure, when we ask them to perform familiar or unfamiliar tasks. We are especially concerned, in this respect, about children who have had no exposure to preschool programs. We do not want to stifle a love of learning when it has barely begun.

We well know the disastrous effects of labeling. Clearly, we want to avoid tagging children with labels that will stick to them for years. The rate of referrals to special education is already far too high in New York City. We want to reverse, rather than promote, this trend. In planning the assessment of our early childhood programs, we are mindful of the potential abuses of testing.

The Effects of Testing on Classroom Experience. Our experience with testing in the later grades makes us tremble a little when we contemplate the task of assessment in our early childhood programs. We are already struggling with the ways in which the imperatives and the limitations of testing distort the educational mission. We are obliged in the schools, even when we deny it, to "teach to the tests," and this means that we give short shrift to many skills and qualities that we value in education because they are not measured in existing standardized tests. The early childhood tests now available vary in the skills they measure, but most are extremely weak in social and emotional development.

Appropriateness. Testing strategies must be appropriate to our goals. We need means of assessment that are broadly based rather than tied to one or two parameters, that will yield more than just a number, and that will measure growth and assess potential in areas such as socialization and self-esteem as well as in cognitive areas.

Our methods must also be appropriate for our own local curriculum and students. Our black and Hispanic parents have a well-founded mistrust of the uses of standardized testing. We will be responsive to their concerns. Research has shown that not all standardized tests are equally appropriate for use with those youngsters who are, in the national context, minorities but who constitute the vast majority of New York City's students (Padilla, 1979; Hilliard, 1979). Our standards of appropriateness must take into account the relevance of test items or tasks not only to the urban experience of our black and Hispanic youngsters but also to the marked cultural and linguistic diversity within these groups.

About 30 percent of children entering our kindergartens speak languages other than English at home (Office of Educational Evaluation, 1983). Most of these children speak Spanish; other large groups speak Chinese (one of several dialects), Haitian Creole, and Russian. In all, students in our schools speak more than forty native languages. This linguistic diversity complicates the problems of identifying appropriate tests and appropriate test givers. Research indicates that simply translating a set of instructions or questions from English into a student's native language does not necessarily result in an appropriate test (Padilla, 1979).

Utility. If we are to meet our public mandate for accountability, our assessments must be usable. The data we collect and distribute must speak to both our short-term and our long-term goals. Data about immediate goals allow school administrators and teachers to make midcourse adjustments to curriculum and services, and they provide parents with meaningful information about student achievement. Data on achievement of long-term goals guide policy planners in revising current strategies and designing new initiatives.

Let me add a few words about the utility of testing in areas other than assessment, since we would hope that the tests we administer to our students would help them and us in other ways as well. Our early childhood teachers need, and often ask for, new kinds of practical instruments that are tied to the realities of the classroom. We are seeking to provide improved diagnostic tools for their use.

We would hope that increased attention to early childhood assessment might reduce the potential for misuse of testing in the early years. In particular, I am concerned about the procedure that has come to be known as "Chapter 53 screening." Mandated by a 1980 New York state law, this screening applies to all children entering the school system and is intended to identify the possibly gifted or possibly handicapped. While laudable in its objective, Chapter 53 screening has come to be viewed as hazardous—particularly in the very early years before a child has become acclimated to the school environment. By developing or adopting more appropriate testing tools for use with our young children, we can help to ensure that no single test, whether norm-referenced or criterion-referenced, serves as the sole means of determining where a child is placed, especially when such a determination may eventually lead to separating the child from the mainstream.

Acceptable Assessment Strategies. Despite the strain on our resources, we must do our best to make our programs work. Despite the great limitations of available testing tools, we must do our best to report on the results of our efforts. In the evaluation of our all-day kindergarten program, we will attempt in several ways to address these difficult accountability problems.

First, in view of the limitations on testing for this age group, we will keep our focus on program assessment, broadly considered, rather than on standardized testing of individual children. Second, we will use the most suitable standardized instruments now available to us so that we can get a sense of how our program is working and so that we can report to the public —and we will proceed with caution. Third, we will supplement test data with descriptive information about our kindergarten children, such as preschool history, attendance patterns, and other available information. Finally, we will, throughout the year, be seeking more reliable and appropriate measurement tools by reviewing standardized tests as well as alternative assessment measures.

In these ways, we will attempt to show how well the program was implemented and whether our kindergarten children are better prepared, as a result of our initiative, to enter the first grade. But we cannot stop here.

We will follow these children. If we are to gauge our success in meeting our more far-reaching goals—preventing failure, reducing the dropout rate, diminishing special education referrals—we must look at the progress of these children up through the grades. Past research has documented the long-term effects of early childhood education (Darlington, 1981; Schweinhart and Weikart, 1980), but additional, more refined longitudinal studies are needed if we are to correct program weaknesses and to ensure program accountability.

Conclusion

We are a public school system. We are held accountable to the public for the services we provide. When we make fundamental changes in the way we educate our children—as we must if we are to move from the current educational mediocrity to the achievement of excellence—we must take care to document what we are doing, and we must spread the word about our efforts and about the results of these efforts.

The public needs to know what we are doing and what results our initiatives are producing. Parents need to know how our policies are affecting their children. Teachers need systematic information about the impact of their efforts. Policy planners need the kind of information that can guide continual improvement of the services we provide to the children of our city.

We owe the public a timely, fair, informative accounting of our performance. At the same time, we must be responsive to the best interests and developmental needs of the children entrusted to us. There should be no conflict between these two unshakable commitments.

The dilemma we face in assessing our youngest pupils presents us with a major challenge. How can we be true to our responsibilities as educators and our integrity as professionals when each step toward the assessment of early childhood programs calls for compromise? We clearly cannot resolve the dilemma alone. We hope that researchers and psyschometricians will share the challenge with us by joining us in our research and development efforts.

The testing community has made strides in refining strategies for measuring growth in the early years. I hope that this important area will receive greater attention from teachers and researchers so that increasingly we can stop misusing testing and start using it effectively.

References

Bissell, J. S. *Implementation of Planned Variation in Head Start.* Washington, D.C.: Office of Child Development, U.S. Department of Health, Education, and Welfare, 1973.

Darlington, R. B. "The Consortium for Longitudinal Studies." *Educational Evaluation and Policy Analysis,* 1981, *3,* 37-45.

Haney, W., and Gelberg, W. *Assessment in Early Childhood Education.* Cambridge, Mass.: The Huron Institute, 1980.

Hilliard, A. G., III. "Standardized Testing and African-Americans: Building Assessor Competence in Systematic Assessment." In *Testing, Teaching, and Learning: Report of a Conference on Research on Testing.* Washington, D.C.: The National Institute of Education, 1979.

House, E. R., and others. "No Simple Answer: Critique of the Follow Through Evaluation." *Harvard Educational Review,* 1978, *48* (2), 128-170.

Lazar, I., and Darlington, R. "Lasting Effects of Early Education: A Report from the Consortium for Longitudinal Studies." *Monographs of the Society for Research in Child Development* (No. 195), 1982, *47*, 2-3.

McClinton, S. L., and Topping, C. *Extended Day Kindergarten: Are the Effects Intangible?* Boulder Valley, Colo.: Boulder Valley Public Schools, 1981.

Nieman, R. H., and Gastright, J. F. *The Long Term Effects of ESEA Title I Preschool and All Day Kindergarten: An Eight Year Follow-Study.* Cincinnati, Ohio: Cincinnati Public Schools, 1981.

Office of Educational Evaluation. *Educational Status of Limited English Proficient Students in New York City Public Schools.* New York: New York City Public Schools, 1983.

Padilla, A. M. "Critical Factors in the Testing of Hispanic Americans: A Review and Some Suggestions for the Future." In *Testing, Teaching, and Learning: Report of a Conference on Research on Testing.* Washington, D.C.: The National Institute of Education, 1979.

Schweinhart, L. J., and Weikart, D. P. *Young Children Grow Up: The Effects of the Perry Preschool Program on Youths Through Age 15.* Ypsilanti, Mich.: High/Scope Educational Research Foundation, 1980.

Systems Development Corporation. *Effects of Different Head Start Program Approaches on Children of Different Characteristics: Report on Analysis of Data From 1968-69 National Evaluation.* Prepared for Project Head Start. Washington, D.C.: Office of Child Development, U.S. Department of Health, Education, and Welfare, 1972.

Winter, M., and Klein, A. E. *Extending the Kindergarten Day: Does It Make a Difference in the Achievement of Educationally Advantaged and Disadvantaged Pupils?* Washington, D.C.: Bureau of Elementary and Secondary Education, U.S. Department of Health, Education, and Welfare, 1970.

5

Value of Standardized Tests in Indicating How Well Students Are Learning

Diane Ravitch

The debate about standardized testing has been one of the most rancorous educational issues of the past decade. Since the case against standardized testing has received a great deal of attention in the popular and scholarly media, the nature of the indictment is by now familiar. Articulate critics have charged that such tests measure only a narrow spectrum of abilities, that the tests by their very nature discourage creative and imaginative thinking, that the results of the tests have far too significant an effect on the life chances of young people, that the emphasis in a multiple-choice test is wrongly on "the right answer" and on simplicity instead of thoughtful judgments, that the tests favor the advantaged over the disadvantaged while claiming to be neutral, and that the tests are inherently biased against those who are unfamiliar with the language and concepts of the majority culture. In short, say the critics, the tests corrupt education, subjugate millions of students to their mechanistic requirements, and limit access to educational opportunity.

In examining the uses and misuses of testing, it is necessary to reflect on this upsurge of hostility to the testing process and to ask why it has occurred now.

My own view is that the tests have become increasingly
controversial because they have become increasingly indispen-
sable. Revulsion against standardized testing has accompanied
the period in which the tests have become a fixture not only in
educational decision making but in entry to the labor market.
One of the forces that underlies the criticism of the tests is egal-
itarianism, for the egalitarian complaint is that the tests discriminate among test takers and favor those with the best education
and the most ability. But the force that makes standardized
testing an omnipresent feature of our society is also egalitarian-
ism, because testing continues to be the most objective mecha-
nism available to allocate benefits. In education, tests have
grown more important to the extent that other measures have
been discarded or discredited. Although it is easy to forget the
past, we should recall that the tests helped to replace an era in
which many institutions of higher education made their selections with due regard to the student's race, religion, class, and
family connections. For many years, the objectivity of the tests
was believed to be the best guarantee that selections would be
made on the basis of ability rather than status.

The tests have assumed an exceptional importance in college admissions, because other measures have been rendered use-
less. Personal recommendations today carry far less weight than
they once did, because letter writers can no longer rely on the
confidentiality of their statements. High school grades are a
questionable standard, not only because of the variability from
one school to another, but because of the prevalence of grade
inflation. If almost everyone applying for admission presents an
A record, then the grade-point average becomes meaningless in
the admission process. In the current situation, the students
who selected demanding courses and the schools that resisted
grade inflation are handicapped when colleges attach importance to the grade-point average. Personal interviews are helpful, but they are limited in value by the interviewer's prejudices
and the student's ability to present himself. When all of these
factors are considered, the tests—despite all their flaws—are left
as the fairest measure of a student's academic ability.

Thus the contemporary paradox: The more egalitarian

our society becomes, the more important standardized tests are. Yet the more important the tests are, the more they are subject to egalitarian criticism for assuming too much power in determining future life chances. As long as there are educational institutions where there are more applicants than places, there must be an objective way to decide who gets in. This being so, the egalitarian critique of testing founders precisely because no other objective means has been discovered to take the place of ability testing.

Unless some more objective means is devised, testing will continue to be pervasive, perhaps even more than it is now. This is not necessarily a development to be welcomed, since it goes hand in hand with the growing bureaucratization of American education. However, it is important to note that the influence of standardized testing in college admissions is limited by demographic factors. Although critics frequently complain about the unconstrained power of the testers, a recent survey by the College Board showed that fewer than 10 percent of all institutions of higher education are highly selective. Most colleges and universities accept all prospective students who apply or require only that they meet minimal standards. Therefore, for the overwhelming majority of students, the tests are used for placement, not for exclusion from educational opportunity.

While they are certainly not perfect instruments of assessment or prediction, tests have appropriate uses for students, teachers, and educational institutions. Students who take the Preliminary Scholastic Aptitude Test (PSAT) or the Scholastic Aptitude Test (SAT), for example, get a measure of their strengths and weaknesses relative to other students. Correctly read, not as a life sentence but as a one-shot assessment of verbal and mathematical abilities, the test scores can direct the student toward appropriate study to improve the areas of academic weakness. For teachers and schools, the tests are useful as rough indicators of how well students are learning the specific skills that are tested. The test scores can help the school in diagnosing educational problems and in prescribing appropriate remedies.

In my own view, the chief virtue of the standardized test

is that it may serve as an early warning system. If a student scores a 350 on the SAT, counselors and teachers should be alerted to find out why and to do something about it. If a school administrator sees a steady downward trend in the scores for a school or a district, it should also be considered a warning of possible problems in the teaching of academic skills.

The best example of how the tests function as an early warning system occurred during the past several years. In 1975, the College Board revealed that SAT scores had steadily declined since 1964. More than any other single factor, the problem of falling test scores stimulated a national debate about education policies. Suddenly, the public and policy makers became concerned about the decline of academic standards and literacy.

Initially, some in the educational field tried to explain away the score decline, either by questioning the validity of the SAT or by pointing to the increased numbers of minority students in the pool of test takers. These attempts to allay public concern were soon rebutted, however, as additional research provided evidence that other standardized tests of verbal skills showed the same pattern of falling scores over the same period. In particular, David Wiley and Annette Harnischfeger's article, "Achievement Test Score Decline: Do We Need to Worry?" (CEMREL, 1975) documented a parallel drop in scores in a wide variety of tests, beginning in about the fifth grade.

The second claim—that the score decline was caused by the inclusion of large numbers of poor and minority students in the test cohort—was effectively dismissed by the blue-ribbon panel appointed by the College Board and chaired by Willard Wirtz. The Wirtz panel found that the new students had contributed to the decline until about 1970; after that date, the composition of the test-taking population had stabilized, yet the SAT averages continued to fall.

The report of the Wirtz panel identified a number of in-school practices that probably contributed to the score decline. It observed that absenteeism, grade inflation, and social promotion had become widespread, while the assignment of homework had shrunk. One of its internal studies, prepared by Harvard reading expert Jeanne Chall, found that the verbal content of widely used high school textbooks had been reduced by as much as two grade levels. Although the panel was careful not to pin the blame for the score decline on any particular factor, it did note that there was "almost certainly some causal relationship between the shift in the high schools from courses in the traditional disciplines to newer electives." It further pointed out that its "firmest conclusion is that the critical factors in the relationship between curricular change and the SAT scores are (1) that less thoughtful and critical reading is now being demanded and done, and (2) that careful writing has apparently about gone out of style."

The SAT score decline sounded a national warning bell that something was terribly wrong in the schools. The reaction was not long in coming, and it was not always wisely considered. In almost every discipline, teachers reported the pressures of a "back-to-basics" movement that demanded greater attention to basic skills and viewed innovative practices with skepticism. Within five years after the news of the score decline broke, nearly forty state legislatures had adopted minimum competency tests in an effort to restore value to the high school diploma. In response to public concern, more than two dozen commissions, task forces, and study panels were established to examine the problems of American education, with special focus on the high schools.

The spring of 1983 saw the release of reports from four of these groups, and several more followed in the fall of the same year. For the first time in a generation, the public became deeply concerned about the problems of American education. Hardly a day went by without an article in the news about merit pay, teacher education, curricular change, tightened standards for high school graduation or college admission, or some other educational subject that a year earlier would not have made it into the papers, let alone onto the agenda of the state legislature.

This time of ferment and reform was directly stimulated by the impact of the SAT score decline. No other single indicator had the power to alert the public that educational quality was slipping nationally or the power to elicit research that identified specific problem areas in the schools. Although one would wish it were possible to generate interest in educational reform without developing so drastic a symptom, nonetheless the SAT score drop dramatically raised the level of public attention to educational problems.

These then are the uses of well-made standardized tests: as an assessment tool to help individual students identify their strengths and weaknesses, as a diagnostic and prescriptive technique to improve individualized learning programs, as a yardstick to help competitive colleges select their students, as a barometer to gauge the learning of academic skills, and as an early warning system to measure national trends in learning these skills.

But the tests, needless to say, are not an unmixed blessing. Many of the criticisms that have been made of them are on the mark. The tests can easily be misused and become an end in themselves rather than a means. It is true that standardized tests measure only a narrow spectrum of abilities and that they cannot measure many valuable ways of thinking. The tests have validity only because the narrow spectrum of abilities that they do measure tend to be central to the learning process in college. The odds favor the future academic success of the student who scores 700 over the student who scores 400, yet the odds are not always right. We all know students who do not test well, who freeze up in the test situation, or who have gifts that the tests do not measure. Sensible admissions officers know this and are on the lookout for youngsters who have the imagination, creativity, or drive that does not register on the SAT.

The critics also have a point when they speak of the simplistic thinking that multiple-choice questions promote. While it is true that many questions asked on the SAT and on achievement tests have only one correct answer among those presented, the very emphasis on the one right answer may itself be educationally counterproductive. As an historian, I am aware that the more I know, the less I am sure of. I am troubled when one of my children is asked to give the three reasons for the outbreak of some war or the four causes of some movement. When the event or movement in question is still being debated by historians, as almost everything is, then I am especially annoyed by the idea that test makers and teachers should treat them as settled issues. As a parent, I want my children to see history, politics, literature, and art in relation to one another and not as compartmentalized events that can be defined in short answers or in multiple-choice questions. Further, I want them to learn that most questions cannot be answered with a "yes" or a "no," that most judgments must be hedged by qualifications, and that questions about literature and history usually require complicated answers that must be explained, justified, and defined. In a better world, educational testers would value the slow, thoughtful response over the fast, reflexive answer.

Overreliance on standardized testing may be dangerous to the health of education. It is certainly dangerous to the integrity of the high school curriculum. The introduction of the SAT, which (in its verbal component) is curriculum-free, left many high schools without a good argument for requiring students to take history, literature, science, or anything not specifically demanded by the college of their choice. The old College Boards were based on a very specific curriculum and on specific works of literature and periods of history; the elite secondary schools agreed on what was important to teach, and their students were well prepared for the examinations, which relied heavily on essay answers. It was a move toward democratic admissions when the SAT was adopted, because the SAT tested scholastic aptitude and made no assumptions about what curriculum the student had studied. As a result, public school students all over the country were able to compete fairly for places in the prestigious colleges. Unlike the authors of the College Entrance Examinations, the makers of the SAT do not care whether the student has ever read Jane Austen or Charles Dickens or any particular work.

Now, it is not the fault of Educational Testing Service that students may arrive at college with high test scores and appallingly little substantive knowledge of history or literature. But the curriculum-free SAT has presented no impediment to high schools that thoughtlessly decimated their own curricular requirements. Because the SAT is curriculum-free, students who are good test takers are justified in thinking that they can do very well in the admission process even if their preparation for college has been haphazard. Again, I want to stress that the SAT did not cause the curricular chaos that has come to be the bane of American high schools. But any admissions officer who relies on SAT scores without scrutinizing the content of the student's high school course work is gravely misusing the test.

Standardized tests are misused when teachers, textbook publishers, curriculum planners, and administrators permit ordinary classroom practice to be dominated by the fill-in-the-blanks mentality, to the virtual exclusion of writing. Researchers have reported increasing time spent in elementary schools and in high schools on workbooks and busywork. The study of textbooks by Jeanne Chall for the Wirtz panel observed a marked increase in emphasis on "objective answers." Chall found that "generally, the assignments in the Reading, History and Literature textbooks (ask) only for underlining, circling, and filling in of single words." When these busywork activities are substituted for student writing, they are anti-intellectual and subversive of good learning. Filling in the blanks is not equivalent educationally to the intellectual chores involved in writing an essay, in which the student must think through what he wants to say, must organize his thoughts, must choose his words with care, and must present his thoughts with precision.

The harm in minimizing the practice of writing in the classroom is not merely to the student; teachers are also injured. Workbook activity requires minimal skill and thought by teachers; they become technicians, checking for the correct answer, a rather low-grade form of labor. When they teach writing, their own intelligence and judgment and skill are brought into play. In order to teach writing, they must make decisions, they must provide guidance, they must set standards of accomplishment. In short, they must wear the mantle of professionalism. The shift in the classroom from teacher control to materials control no doubt contributes to what observers have called the "de-skilling" or the "technicization" of teaching, a process that converts teachers from professionals to civil servants.

In sum, there can be no doubt that the tests have their uses as well as their misuses. The standardized test must always be seen as a measuring device, an assessment tool, never as an end in itself. The skills that it measures are important, but it does not measure every important skill. The information that it gives us about the state of a student's learning is never definitive but only tentative and subject to future change. Above all, we should not permit the standardized test to become the be-all and end-all of educational endeavor; we send our children to school not to do well on tests but to become educated people, knowledgeable about the past and the present and prepared to continue learning in the future. Tests help us check up on how well children are learning, and this is their major value. Their uses are clear and limited. The mastery of tests should not be permitted to fill in the blank of what should be our educational philosophy.

Those who believe in the value of tests have a particular responsibility to guard against their misuse—in the classroom, the press, admissions offices, and the workplace.

6

Responding to Charges of Test Misuse in Higher Education

Fred A. Hargadon

The theme of this book focuses on the uses and misuses of tests. The comments I have to offer reflect my experience as an admissions dean for the past eighteen years, during which time I have actually made use of such tests as the Scholastic Aptitude Test (SAT), Achievement Tests, Test of English as a Foreign Language (TOEFL), and Advanced Placement tests offered by the College Board in the undergraduate admissions processes at two particular institutions, Swarthmore College and Stanford University.

John Casteen began his remarks with a sixteenth-century folk tale. My remarks are most appropriately begun, I think, by recalling the escapades of Milo, the young man in Norton Juster's (1972) delightful *The Phantom Tollbooth,* a twentieth-century children's book written for adults (or is it the other way around?). Thinking he has found the city of Reality, Milo is corrected by his guide, Alec.

> "Oh no, that's only Illusions," said Alec. "The real city is over there."
> "What are Illusions?" Milo asked, for it was the loveliest city he'd ever seen.

"Illusions," explained Alec, "are like mirages," and, realizing that this didn't help much, he continued: "And mirages are things that aren't really there that you can see very clearly."

"How can you see something that isn't there?" yawned the Humbug, who wasn't fully awake yet.

"Sometimes it's much simpler than seeing things that are," he said. "For instance, if something is there, you can only see it with your eyes open, but if it isn't there, you can see it just as well with your eyes closed. That's why imaginary things are often easier to see than real ones" [pp. 115–116].

To many of us who actually use tests, the claims of the critics that tests are used with a false sense of precision, or without regard to their limitations, all too often appear to be based on *imagined* use rather than on the actual use to which they are put.

Some Factors Affecting the Usefulness of the SAT and Other Tests

I think tests are useful. I think the degree of usefulness varies from one institution to another. I think they can be, and sometimes are, used unwisely. And I think it is no more unwise to weigh them too heavily than it is to accord them too little weight.

It has been my experience that arguments over the manner in which tests are used are frequently, at heart, arguments over their usefulness. And, arguments over their usefulness are frequently, in essence, arguments over educational goals, objectives, and philosophies and/or social values, distributive justice, and the like.

This is why it turns out to be far easier to acknowledge the possibility of tests being misused than it is to both document and gain consensus on actual instances of misuse. It is not at all clear, for example, as we are so frequently asked to assume, that when a student fails to gain admission to institution "X" and goes on to do well at institution "Y," and when that student's test results may have contributed to the decision by institution "X" to deny admission, we therefore have *prima-facie* evidence of test misuse.

From my perspective, arguments over the usefulness of tests all too often seem to be characterized by one or more of the following weaknesses:

- The tendency to draw broad conclusions from relatively few cases, frequently anecdotal in nature.
- An almost complete lack of detailed descriptions of the *actual* uses to which tests are put by the thousands of individual institutions of higher education in this country.
- The tendency to treat test usage in all institutions of higher education similarly without differentiating among institutions.
- The tendency to treat the applicability of validity studies in a similarly undifferentiated manner.
- The tendency to treat validity studies solely as a commentary on the strengths and weaknesses of the tests rather than also considering them a possible commentary on the strengths and weaknesses of grades and grading systems.
- The tendency to frame arguments in an all-or-nothing form; for example, tests are either useful or they are not or tests are either misused or they are not. The rhetoric too often appears to require that one abjure such qualifiers as "sometimes" or "some."

Common sense suggests that the usefulness of tests, and the usefulness of just about every other instrument used in assessing the likelihood of a given student's level of success in a collegiate academic program, will vary not only from institution to institution but within the same institution. This will depend, in the former instance, on the different educational philosophies and goals that characterize the many different kinds of institutions of higher education in this country and, in the latter instance, on the different kinds of intellectual skills and academic preparation required by different departments and schools within a single institution.

Common sense also suggests that the usefulness of a given

test (the SAT, for example) will vary, depending on the purposes for which it is being used: admission, placement, longitudinal tracking of the various dimensions of applicant pools and/ or enrolled student cohorts, scholarship competitions, and so forth.

It follows that a given college may find that the use of such a test as the SAT will turn out to be of little value in predicting academic performance at that particular college. Or, even if such tests are useful in predicting academic performance at that college, sheer academic performance (as measured by grades) may not be accorded the highest value among a hierarchy of characteristics deemed most desirable for that college's student body by its faculty. Some institutions, on the other hand, may place a premium on sheer academic performance as measured by grades and may also find the use of such tests as the SAT to be of value in predicting that performance, either for individual students or for a student body as a whole.

The results of a validity study at institution "X" may or may not be applicable to institution "Y." The fact that students with average SAT scores in the 400s graduate in the top 10 percent of the class at institution "X" does not mean they would graduate in the top 10 percent of the class at institution "Y." For all sorts of reasons, academic standards vary from institution to institution, from department to department within a given institution, and from one faculty member to another in the same department. This hardly constitutes news, except that the caveats it suggests, which ought to be employed by those who use the validity studies from a *given* institution in order to attack the usefulness of tests for *all* such institutions, are in fact so rarely acknowledged.

The failure to differentiate among institutions of higher education accounts for the remarkable assertion by Boyer (1983) in his recent book on high schools, to the effect that "The SAT is not very helpful in predicting how a student is likely to do in college" (p. 133). While that opinion is mildly qualified in the succeeding sentences, its conclusive rendering is not. What is most striking is that in a very illuminating report, which appears to be otherwise scrupulously documented and footnoted, Boyer's remarks about the usefulness of the SAT rather uncharacteristically lack not only any supporting evidence but even any reference to supporting evidence.

Not surprisingly, at a meeting I attended shortly after this report was released, someone stated as fact that the "SAT is not very helpful," citing, as authority, Boyer. As will inevitably happen, of course, Boyer's assertion will be cited by others as fact, documented, of course, by an appropriate reference to "Boyer (1983), p. 133," a source that all too few will take the time to trace and discover that the original assertion itself lacks any documentation.

There are several respects in which the traditional validity studies, at least in some cases, may actually underestimate the usefulness of such tests as the SAT.

With respect to my own experience in admissions, Manski and Wise (1983, pp. 16, 17) come much closer to the mark than does Boyer in commenting on the possible usefulness of the SAT. From the evidence they gathered, which is set out in their book, they concluded:

> Much of the recent criticism (of the SAT) is based on interpretation of the findings of validity studies of SAT tests that emphasize correlations between test scores and/or class rank on the one hand and college grades on the other. Validity studies and the interpretations of their findings also by implication emphasize the effect of test scores on college admissions decisions, while largely ignoring their relationship to student choices; and they ignore student persistence decisions, which may be the single most important indicator of success in college. *Furthermore, they are invariably limited to relationships within a single college or university. Both self-selection by students and decisions of admissions officers tend to minimize the relationship between test scores and performance among students in a single college or university.* [Emphasis added.]

In other words, the true validity of the SAT in predicting academic performance, at least in some instances, is attenuated, first by student self-selection and then by college admissions decisions, resulting in clusters of relatively high-scoring students at some institutions and relatively low-scoring students at others, institutions of both types distributing the same grades in roughly the same manner and each graduating class with a top 10 percent and a bottom 90 percent.

I am inclined to think that the true validity of the SAT also may have been attenuated in recent years in at least two other respects. For instance, I have a hunch that the usefulness of tests like the SAT in a given institution may depend on, among other things, the size of that institution.

A large institution with many classes numbering in the hundreds, and where the students are relatively anonymous, is not as likely to take into account in its awarding of grades as many personal elements as may be considered at a very small institution where instructors may personally know every student in their classes. This is not necessarily the case in either instance, of course, but it would be hard to deny that it happens and that it can have an effect on the degree to which tests prove useful in predicting academic performance in the respective institutions.

In addition, in the last decade many colleges and universities, including my own, Stanford University, dismantled what had previously been a more or less common curriculum for their freshman classes. Consequently, up until recently, the number of different kinds of courses freshmen could (and did) take numbered in the hundreds.

Accordingly, it is possible (and I happen to think it to be the case) that the wider range of course choices allowed freshmen in the past decade made it easier for *all* students to find more courses in which they could be assured of doing well, thereby accounting, in some measure, not only for the grade inflation that took place during that time, but also for the possible attenuation of the results of validity studies conducted during that period.

When all of this is taken into consideration along with the problems of comparability of grades, it raises some questions about whether the true value of the SAT may not, in fact, have been underestimated by the traditional validity studies correlating it with academic performance in the freshman year.

When one considers all the institutions of higher education in this country, nothing even comes close to being as influential in determining college admissions as applicants' high school transcripts and grades (Hargadon, 1981). Given this fact, it never ceases to amaze me that grades and grading systems, characterized as they are by incomparability from school to school, department to department, course to course, and teacher to teacher, generate so little heat and controversy, especially when compared to that which surrounds the use of national standardized examinations.

When one considers the inflation in grading (at both the school and college levels) that accompanied the decline in performance on just about every set of state and national standardized examinations over the past decade and a half, one is bound to wonder whether it is not precisely the inherent flexibility (even manipulability) of grades that enabled them to be awarded in such a fashion as to mute potential criticism, to keep to a minimum the number of hassles with students and parents, and to lead those in the schools to argue that grades ought to be given much greater weight than test scores in college admissions.

Test Scores As Supplementary Evidence
for Admission Purposes

In my own institution we find tests to be a useful supplementary piece of evidence to take into consideration when attempting to get a fix on the relative academic abilities and preparation of our applicants for admission. Like most admissions processes, I imagine, ours is one that represents a compromise between, on the one hand, gathering as much evidence as we possibly can about each and every applicant (short of living with them for a year) and, on the other hand, what it is reasonable to expect the applicants can and will provide us and what we also can reasonably expect we can sift and evaluate in a limited amount of time.

Why use the results of the SAT, as we do, as one such

piece of evidence? First, because in a given year our 14,000 or so applicants for freshman admission will come from almost 5,000 different secondary schools, perhaps only half of which are schools from which we receive applicants on a regular basis.

One need not immerse oneself, as I do, in the daily process of attempting to square a given applicant's A+ in English and accompanying laudatory letter of recommendation from the English teacher with that same applicant's self-testimonial to the effect that he or she has been asked to "tudor (sic) the slower students in English," to worry over the proper weight to be accorded that particular student's grade in English. (Alas, such examples run into the thousands.) Frankly, we consider grades (like test scores) a necessary but insufficient piece of evidence in assessing a student's academic abilities and preparation.

Moreover, one should keep in mind that there is some merit in predicting the academic performance of an entering class even when one cannot be certain of the performance of every member in it. I am reminded of the founder of life insurance who is said to have remarked that "while there is nothing so unpredictable as the life of a single individual, there is nothing so predictable as the lives of a thousand."

Second, I am inclined to agree with David Riesman that some form of national standardized test may in fact free some students from the "personalism" of school authorities and parents (Willingham, Breland, and Associates, 1977). Admissions officers are properly as wary of the credentials of the most popular student, who can do no wrong, as they are of the credentials of an unpopular student, who can do no right.

Third, the results of such tests as the Achievement Tests (which my own institution recommends but does not require) or the advanced placement (AP) examinations provide students with the opportunity to indicate exceptionally well-honed competencies in one or more subject fields (thereby adding credibility to a student's high grade in a particular subject or giving us reason to overlook a student's modest grade in a given subject. Such test results also can have the opposite effect, leading us to question, for instance, how a given student with straight A's in math can score no more than 350 on the Math Achievement exam).

Fourth, when a student is applying from a school with which we have little or no familiarity, particularly when, from what we can gather, it is not a particularly demanding school, that student's test results may provide us with the necessary confidence or the necessary leverage we need to make an admissions decision, either positive or negative, that we consider to be as much in that student's best interest as in our own.

It should be obvious from the following tables (for the class of 1987) that my own institution does not admit students simply on the basis of test scores. Since, when evaluating applications, we treat the verbal and math SAT scores separately (if the student has taken the test more than once, the scores we record are the highest achieved), Table 1 presents the two scores separately.

Table 1. Applicants/Admits, Class of 1987, by Separate SAT Scores.

Verbal SAT	Number of Applicants	Number Offered Admission	Math SAT	Number of Applicants	Number Offered Admission
700–800	1,014	498	700–800	3,618	1,116
600–699	3,772	1,075	600–699	4,906	965
500–599	4,498	714	500–599	2,792	324
Below 500	3,148	169	Below 500	1,066	51

Note: Applicants submitting ACT scores, which we also accept, are not included in these tables.

Table 2 is an applicant/admit table showing composite scores (that is, total of highest verbal and highest math scores).

Taking yield into account (that is, the percentage of those offered admission who decide to enroll), had we simply admitted by test scores, we could have filled the freshman class with students whose composite scores all would have been above 1350.

The second piece of evidence we take into account when assessing applicants' academic abilities and preparation is their

Table 2. Applicants/Admits, Class of 1987, by Total SAT Scores.

SAT Total	Number of Applicants	Number Offered Admission
1600–1500	209	123
1499–1400	1102	504
1399–1300	2382	723
1299–1200	2854	550
1199–1100	2441	334
1099–1000	1735	164
999–900	908	45
899–800	420	11
Below 800	193	2

grades. In calculating the grade-point average (GPA) for each applicant, we count only the traditional academic courses (what we refer to as "solids"). Such adjusted GPAs, then, are the ones represented in Table 3.

Table 3. Applicants/Admits, Class of 1987, by High School GPA.

High School GPA	Number of Applicants	Number Offered Admission
4.0	2,212	874
3.9	1,113	338
3.8	1,436	353
3.7	1,135	241
3.6	958	142
3.5 and below	4,663	458

It should be equally obvious from Table 3 that we also do not admit simply by GPA. Had we so desired, we could have filled the freshman class with 4.0 students. In many cases, those with lower GPAs in Table 3 who were offered admission represent, for the most part, students whose academic programs were at least as rigorous as, and very frequently more rigorous than, those of many with higher GPAs. Just as there are great differences in the course loads represented by identical GPAs, so too, are there still a number of secondary schools where the grading is quite rigorous and where the top student will have no more than a 3.5 GPA.

A third piece of evidence we take into account has to do with the number of solids a student has taken in high school and the number of those that are honors or AP courses. In large measure, it is this particular piece of evidence that accounts for the relatively broad distribution of GPAs and test scores represented by those offered admission in the tables above. We encourage students to take a rigorous program in high school. As one might deduce from the preceding table, our decisions do not reward those who have achieved a high GPA by taking a light program. (We do, of course, take into account that a light program may represent the most difficult program a given school offers. We ask ourselves about each application we evaluate, "How well has the student used the resources available?")

Basically, we pull these three pieces of evidence together to assign academic ratings to each applicant. The ratings are approximate ones. The highest rating is a "1," and the lowest a "5." A typical "1" would be an applicant whose test scores are in the 700+ range, who has taken at least twenty semester solids in the tenth and eleventh grades and an additional five in the first semester of the senior year, who has taken a significant number of AP or honors courses, and who has a 4.0 GPA (or equivalent, depending on the rigorousness of the school's grading system). A typical "2" would have test scores all in the 650-700 range, who has taken eighteen to twenty semester solids in the tenth and eleventh grades and an additional four or five in the first semester of the senior year, who has taken some AP and honors courses, and has a 3.9 (or equivalent GPA). The lowest academic rating is a "5," which includes all applicants with credentials that place them somewhere from just below a "4" on down to those with the least impressive set of credentials. Approximately half of our applicants in a given year are rated "4" and above. Obviously, not all applicants easily fit into the typical examples I have cited.

We arrive at considered judgments about whether a given applicant's credentials merit, say, a "1" rating or a "2." There are, of course, gray zones between ratings. There are cases where the distinction between a "1" and a "2" or between a "2" and a "3" are blurred, but the distinctions between a "1" and a "3" or between a "2" and a "4" are clear. (When one groups "1" and "2" together, that is a fair approximation of the top quarter of our applicants, and groups "3" and "4" together are a fair approximation of the second quarter of our applicants, based solely on academic credentials.) All of this is relative to our particular applicant group, of course, given that many of our "5s" are in fact quite able and solid students who could successfully pursue the academic program at any college in the country, including Stanford.

It should be clearly stated that these ratings do not by themselves dictate our admissions decisions. We assign the ratings for a variety of reasons. First, they enable us to get a handle on sorting our applicants in terms of their relative academic credentials. Second, by having an academic rating system that does not take into account either the nonacademic parts of applications or the nonquantifiable aspects of assessments, it enables us to be more aware of just when factors other than academic credentials are being taken into account when making our decisions. Third, it provides us with a system by which to track changes in the nature of the academic credentials of our applicant groups, and enrolled freshman classes, from year to year.

To the academic ratings are added our evaluations of all other parts of the students' applications: their self-presentation (including essays), recommendations from their schools and teachers, evidence of particularly well-developed skills or competencies (be they academic, musical, athletic, or artistic in nature), their work experience, any handicaps or disadvantages with which they have had to cope, and their life experiences in general. All such factors are taken into consideration together with applicants' academic credentials when making admissions decisions.

Our admissions policy (and the decisions based on it) is partly dictated by our being a residential university, where all freshmen are required to live on campus (approximately 85 percent of all undergraduates live on campus) and the fact that we believe that the education of each student is significantly enhanced by that student's being part of a student body that, while academically able, is also characterized by diversity in terms of the backgrounds, life experiences, ambitions, career goals, and the like of its various members.

Our admissions policy also reflects the fact that at our particular institution freshmen are not admitted to a given department or school. All entering freshmen have until the end of their sophomore year to declare a major.

While an academic rating of "1" does not guarantee admission and an academic rating of "5" does not guarantee being turned down, it is true that the probabilities of admission, all other things being equal, are related to the academic ratings. The higher the rating, the better the odds of being admitted. And, as one would expect, our yield on applicants admitted has an inverse relationship to our academic ratings. We admit a higher percentage of academic "1s" than of any other academic rating, and because they are also the ones most likely to be offered admission everywhere else, our yield is lowest in that category. For all sorts of reasons (but not, as popular lore would have it, primarily for alumni or athletic reasons), we offer admission to students in all five categories (even though we could fill the freshman class with academic 1s and 2s alone). It is simply that once we have determined relative academic ability and preparation, we then apply judgments with regard to other factors, such as those mentioned above. We do not admit anyone who we think does not have a reasonable prospect of successfully completing our academic program.

We inform prospective applicants before they apply that we do not base our decisions solely on GPA or test scores and that there are some factors not under their control when applying for admission, namely, the number and quality of all other applicants in a given year and the choices we exercise in attempting to enroll a freshman class that is both able and diverse.

We do not attempt to predict first-year performance, at least partly for reasons I have alluded to above. (In fact, we have very little academic attrition.) We are much more interested in looking at each senior class as it graduates and in checking to see what academic ratings we had originally assigned to those who graduate Phi Beta Kappa, with Distinction or Honors, or in Tau Beta Pi (the Engineering honor society), more or less to see if we have the academic rating system upside down. It appears we do not. The probabilities of our students gaining these kinds of recognition by graduation clearly are significantly related to the academic ratings assigned them when they applied for admission. We happily admit "3s," "4s," and "5s," but it turns out to be a long shot for any of them to achieve the kinds of academic distinctions mentioned above. (Interestingly, our four Rhodes Scholars in the past two years were all academic "1s.") All things are relative, however, and many of the students who happen to have academic ratings of "3," "4," or "5," and whom we admit, are, I think, nevertheless among the very ablest in the country.

We think our particular system maximizes a number of objectives for us while, at the same time, keeping academic attrition low and relative achievement high. We recognize those things we cannot be precise about in evaluating applicants. We also recognize that our system would not be appropriate to colleges with different (more specialized or narrower or broader) objectives than our own.

For us, the benefits of our system (including the academic ratings) are two: (1) we consider academic achievement as more than the mere accumulation of a good GPA, and we get a hold on that by closely looking at the nature of the academic program in which a given GPA was achieved, and (2) we are able to obtain a fairly clear picture of what the specific trade-offs are should we attempt to maximize one or another goal or objective in enrolling a freshman class—for example, at what point an effort to increase test score medians or GPA medians would result in a reduction in one or another aspect of diversity.

The point here is not to suggest that our particular system has merit beyond our own institution, but rather to provide more substantive context within which to view my remarks on test use, test usefulness, and test misuse. It should be clear from the information provided above why it is I hear as often from those who think we have misused test scores by according them too little weight as from those who think we have misused them in according them too much weight. It should also be clear that it is precisely our attempt to take into account a host of other nonquantifiable factors when making admissions decisions that evokes at least as much criticism as do those systems for making admissions decisions that are formula based (that is, largely a matter of test scores and GPA in some combination of the two).

How Are Test Scores Misused?

Let me now turn to the question of the misuses of tests. As a trustee of the College Board for the past eleven years, I have been a participant in discussions about the guidelines to be issued about proper and improper uses of test data and related information. The College Board publishes *Guidelines on the Uses of College Board Test Scores and Related Data*. It cautions schools, colleges, counselors, admissions officers, and scholarship agencies about the limitations of test results, about the necessity of informing those who take the tests about what they mean and do not mean, about the necessity of protecting the privacy of test candidates, and about the necessity of using the test results only in conjunction with other evidence such as a student's transcripts and grades and so forth (College Entrance Examination Board, 1981).

More specific than that the guidelines do not get. Understandably, it has been difficult to achieve consensus on such matters as just how much weight ought to be accorded a given test score in a given institution's admission process (for reasons I have indicated in the first section of this paper). And it therefore has been difficult to gain consensus among intelligent and sensitive people about what constitutes misuse of test scores.

When one goes beyond the obvious (for example, test scores are not the measure of the worth of any person), it is extremely difficult in a system of higher education as varied and complex and as all encompassing in educational objectives as is our country's to agree upon a single, specific, and circumscribed use to which such test scores legitimately can be put. Some institutions give college credit for AP scores of 3; others

give credit only for 4s and 5s. Such differences are more likely
to reflect differences in curricula of the respective institutions
than examples of proper use or misuse of the test results.

The situation is compounded by the fact that the public
itself is not of one mind when it comes to what constitutes misuse of test scores. For instance, as I have suggested, those of us
in admissions at institutions like my own just as often find ourselves under fire for giving too little weight to test scores as for
giving too much weight to them. One need not be cynical to
conclude that those with high test scores wish them to be accorded great weight and those with low test scores wish them to
be accorded little weight. It was particularly refreshing to read
an application this past year in which the student's comment
that I would notice his test scores were low, instead of being
followed by the normal proffering of excuses, simply went on
and said: "I think they are accurate."

My own experience suggests that most charges of test
misuse represent nothing more than disappointment over an unfavorable admissions decision. Moreover, in a time when criticism of tests has become a growth industry, the improper use
of test scores has quickly become the rationalization of choice
when attempting to come to grips with unfavorable admissions
decisions.

I now offer a couple of examples of test use that are currently generating controversy and comment on each.

First, there is the recently adopted legislation of the
NCAA, Proposition 48. In a long overdue effort to introduce
minimal academic integrity to collegiate athletics in this country, the National Collegiate Athletic Association (NCAA) has
proposed that only students entering college with at least a 2.0
GPA and a composite SAT score of 700 be eligible to participate in varsity sports during their freshman year of college.
While it is disappointing that it is only the test score and not the
scandalously low GPA that has drawn the fire of critics, it is
not, for reasons I suggested above, surprising. Grades are simply
rarely questioned and, in any event, the required grades for eligibility are rather more easily delivered on demand than the required scores on tests.

I think Proposition 48 represents an unwise and improper use of the SAT scores, however. My main objection has to do with the indiscriminate application of a minimal test score, for purposes of athletic eligibility, to all institutions of higher education. A student with less than a 700 total SAT score might very well have a reasonable chance of successfully completing the academic program at a college where the median SAT scores are in the 800s or 900s. Or, that same student might very well have a reasonable chance of successfully completing a given program within a large university where the median test scores of the majors in that program are in the 800s or 900s, even though the university as a whole has higher median test scores.

As I have argued with regard to the inapplicability of a given validity study at a given institution to all institutions, so too, I argue against applying any sort of minimum test score across all institutions, however reasonable such a minimum test score might be at a given institution.

It seems to me that the NCAA is attempting to solve two particular problems with Proposition 48 (and, incidentally, with Proposition 56, possibly the more significant proposition, which attempts to instill minimal academic integrity into the notion of "normal progress" once a student is enrolled in college). The first problem is that of finding a way to make it more difficult for colleges to simply enroll athletes, regardless of whether there is a reasonable prospect of their ever graduating, in order to use them for four or five years and then discard them without ever having provided them the education (and degree) implied in the institution's charter.

I am not convinced that the suggested minimal test score would enhance the educational prospects of athletes at those institutions, which even now make a mockery of the term student-athlete, despite the fact that their athletes might meet or exceed the proposed minimal standards. I do think there are some institutions in which students with scores lower than the proposed minimum do fall within the mainstream of the student body and do have a realistic chance of successfully pursuing the academic programs, through graduation, of those institutions.

There is a second problem the NCAA is wrestling with, although it never quite surfaces in an explicit way. It has to do with the perceived unfairness that can sometimes result from, and is thought to be inherent in, scheduling of athletic contests between institutions with quite different academic standards (something that we are all too polite to mention despite the fact that there may be quite legitimate reasons for such different academic standards). I do not think the use of minimal SAT scores will solve this particular problem. That is neither the test's intended, nor its proper, use.

The NCAA could devise a formula for eligibility, including the use of test scores, that is more directly related to the probability of a given student successfully completing the academic program of a given college. Such a formula would necessarily be more complex and more difficult to administer than Proposition 48, and it would no doubt be more difficult to monitor. But in fact it would more closely approximate what I take to be the intended goals of the legislation.

Moreover, if at halftime during televised games, instead of running pictures of science labs and buildings that many of those on the field that day might not even recognize, the networks displayed simple tables showing how many scholarship athletes entered each of the two schools four or five years previously, how many graduated, and in what majors, it would have a tremendous impact on both the institutions and prospective student-athletes alike and would put the contest in some perspective.

I would be remiss were I also not to mention another reservation I have about Proposition 48. For many institutions, the proposed 2.0 and total SAT of 700 (or ACT of 15) will seem low (or easily met). In a remarkably insightful article, entitled "Ironies of American Law Enforcement," Bayley makes the point (which agrees with my own experience) that "reliance on formal sanctions undermines the vitality with which groups regulate themselves, both in territorial communities and professional groups." He suggests that we may have come to the point where "legal liberty tends to define the boundaries of moral propriety" (Bayley, 1980, p. 52). The proposed NCAA legislation would provide at least some institutions with a "moral propriety" for seeking to enroll, or continuing to enroll, athletes who meet the NCAA minimal standards but remain out of the academic mainstream of an institution's student body.

Almost as controversial as Proposition 48 has been the use, or proposed use, by colleges of "cutoff" scores for admission. I do not believe that the use of cutoff scores, per se, is a misuse of tests. I think the appropriateness of the use of cutoff scores has to be determined on a case-by-case basis. There are two instances in which I think the use of cutoff scores may be quite appropriate. The first is in those cases where a given institution's research indicates that the probabilities of a student's successfully completing that institution's academic program are greatly diminished if the student enters with test scores below a given point. The second instance is when the demand for admission to an institution is sufficiently high and the applicant group of such quality that the probabilities of gaining admission with a relatively low test score are such that it would be misleading to encourage an application from such a person. In a sense, it is consumer-protectionist to have cutoff scores in either case.

In any event, I do not understand why test cutoffs are, per se, any less desirable than grade cutoffs. It is interesting, is it not, that the recommended test-score cutoff in Proposition 48, and not the recommended grade-point cutoff, fuels controversy over setting a cutoff.

If I am not mistaken, both the NCAA Proposition 48 and the use of cutoff scores are the current centers of controversy over the possible misuse of test scores. I would like to mention one other instance of possible misuse of test scores, though admittedly it is of less than universal interest. A few years ago, a noted educational researcher published an article in which he listed colleges by their degree of selectivity in admissions, the criterion of selectivity being that of the median test scores of their enrolled students. I took exception to the use of test scores in this manner, not only because that particular definition of selectivity is misleading but also because its particular use in that article might encourage institutions with the capability of doing so simply to admit by test scores in order to raise their median test scores and thereby move up on the selectivity index. Naturally, my objections came after the fact and did no good, while the existence of such articles continues to influence, however irrationally, the college choices of students.

Indeed, my own experience suggests that for institutions with applicant groups both sizable (relative to the number who can be offered admission) and relatively uniformly highly qualified, a better measure of selectivity might be the profile of whom they turn down, similar in nature, as you might expect, to the tables I presented earlier.

Finally, there are simply some instances in which I may think a particular use of test scores is unwise but does not constitute what most people have in mind when they use the term *misuse*. A large, public, and first-rate institution near my own uses a formula for admissions that, in effect, represents a sort of balance wheel (or see-saw) between GPA and test scores in determining admission. A student with a low GPA may offset that by having high test scores. In fact, if the test scores are sufficiently high, it does not matter how low the GPA is. Or, extremely low test scores may be offset by a high GPA. At the extremes, this seems to me an unwise use of test scores, in the one instance, and of GPA in the other (although I am more concerned about the former than the latter). But I have yet to bring myself to think of it as a misuse of test scores.

If, in fact, such a system does not result in any lower probability of successful completion of that institution's program for such high-scoring low achievers in high school, as I assume must be the case, then however much I might think it unwise policy (in terms of the signals it sends to students and high schools alike) I do not think it qualifies as a misuse of test scores.

Conclusion

In summary, I think we are in need of more extensive case studies of purported misuse of tests than are presently at hand for examination by the academic community and others, including the critics of tests and their uses. Until such time as such cases are developed, all of us would be well advised to be alert to the possibility of such misuses as well as to the possibility that a given charge of misuse may be at heart nothing more than an expression of disappointment over the results of the use to which a test has quite properly been put.

References

Bayley, D. C. "Ironies of American Law Enforcement." *The Public Interest,* 1980, *59,* 45-56.

Boyer, E. L. *High School: A Report on Secondary Education in America.* New York: Harper & Row, 1983.

College Entrance Examination Board. *Guidelines on the Uses of College Board Test Scores and Related Data.* New York: College Entrance Examination Board, 1981.

Hargadon, F. "Tests and College Admissions." *American Psychologist,* 1981, *36* (10), 1113-1116.

Juster, N. *The Phantom Tollbooth.* New York: Random House, 1972.

Manski, C. F., and Wise, D. A. *College Choice in America.* Cambridge, Mass.: Harvard University Press, 1983.

Willingham, W. W., Breland, H. M., and Associates. "The Status of Selective Admissions." In Carnegie Council on Policy Studies in Higher Education, W. M. Manning, W. W. Willingham, and H. M. Breland and Associates, *Selective Admissions in Higher Education: Comment and Recommendations and Two Reports.* San Francisco: Jossey-Bass, 1977.

7

How Test Results
Affect College Admissions
of Minorities

Franklyn G. Jenifer

Among the standardized tests widely used by institutions of higher education as part of their admission processes are a series of tests, such as the Scholastic Aptitude Test (SAT), the Graduate Record Examinations (GRE), the Law School Admission Test (LSAT), and the Graduate Management Admission Test (GMAT), administered by Educational Testing Service (ETS) and controlled by associations of colleges and graduate and professional schools.

Despite the nearly universal use of the results of these tests by four-year colleges and universities, they have been attacked by critics as not being valid indicators for predicting a student's future academic performance. The most publicized and comprehensive commentary of which I am aware was a report written by Nairn and Associates (1980). In addition, several of these tests have been criticized by black psychologists (Williams, 1971) and community leaders as being racially biased.

What I find interesting about the ensuing public debate is that supporters of the tests claim the tests have played a major role in democratizing the process of admission to institutions of higher education, while those who oppose their use claim such tests constitute formidable barriers to democratizing the admission process. If we can explain the bases for these contradictory views, we will be in a better position to evaluate the validity of the criticisms directed against these tests.

Historical Perspective

Higher education began in this country more than 300 years ago with the founding of Harvard and the other eight prerevolutionary colonial colleges. By the early nineteenth century, a small group of colleges founded largely by religious groups or wealthy individuals was educating an elite student clientele. Later in the nineteenth century, with the coming of research and graduate programs based on the German model and with the establishment of the Land Grant colleges, both the mission and size of the American system of higher education expanded rapidly. Yet those who needed and could afford a collegiate education still did not include many women, black Americans, or poor immigrant white Americans.

It was not until the twentieth century that advocates of a more egalitarian society began to argue that a collegiate education should not be a birthright but an earned right of those who have demonstrated their ability to benefit from college. Because school grades and other information traditionally used in making collegiate admission decisions were not comparable from student to student, institutions of higher education increasingly adopted the use of standardized admission tests as a supplement. These were intended to provide a common, reliable, and fair means of assessing relative student ability or merit.

As soon as the principle of granting admission to applicants on the basis of merit was adopted, the use of these tests played an important role in making higher education accessible to a significant portion of our citizens who had previously been denied admission because of their low socioeconomic class or gender. The chief benefactors were first-generation immigrants. This democratization of higher education, which occurred immediately after World War II, was largely responsible, in my opinion, for the extraordinary improvement in the quality of intellectual life that marked American society during this period.

However, black Americans and certain other minorities did not benefit to the same extent from the use of standardized admission tests. On the contrary, since their performance on these tests is consistently below that of white Americans, the use of these tests has acted as a substantial barrier to access to higher education for minorities in general and black Americans specifically.

Significance of Testing on Admission Philosophies

Equal Opportunity Admission. The differential impact standardized testing has had on the accessibility of higher education to poor immigrants on the one hand and blacks and other minorities on the other has created a major split in America concerning collegiate, professional, and graduate school admission philosophy. Our nation is committed to ensuring each citizen, regardless of race, gender, or socioeconomic status, an equal opportunity for access to a higher education. This equal opportunity is achieved, in its purest form, by ensuring that no one is denied the chance to go to college because of inability to pay, and by requiring that each institution of higher education take positive action to increase the size and diversity of its pool of applicants for admissions but restrict the number of applicants actually admitted using criteria that measure ability (merit). Since standardized tests are the single most powerful tool available for measuring ability accurately, objectively, and with comparability, they are the instruments of choice. I will refer to such admission processes and similar modified versions as equal opportunity admission. Despite its many obvious virtues, equal opportunity admission is de facto discriminatory against blacks and other minority Americans.

Affirmative Action Admission. We as a nation are also equally aware and concerned about the findings of the National Advisory Commission on Civil Disorders (1968), which are as valid today as they were then. The commission stated the following as a basic conclusion of its study: "Our nation is moving toward two societies—one black, one white—separate and unequal" (p. 1). Furthermore, the commission warned, "To pursue our present course will involve the continuing polarization of the American community and ultimately the destruction of democratic values" (p. 1). To avoid this, the commission suggested "a commitment to national action—compassionate, massive and sustained, backed by the resources of the most powerful and richest nation on earth" (p. 1).

If we as a nation want to close the socioeconomic gap that separates whites from blacks in America, we must invest heavily in the human capital of the black community. Education is the most important investment because it is a key determinant of future earnings. Thus, increasing access to higher education for black and other minority Americans must be a central goal of public policy in America. The most rapid means of accomplishing this would be the widespread use of admission policies that I will call affirmative action admission. This is similar to equal opportunity admission in that positive action to increase the size and diversity of the applicant pool is mandated; however, it differs from equal opportunity admission in that, once the pool of applicants has been established, *race* is used as a factor in admission decisions. The most extreme version of affirmative action admission would be the establishment of quotas for admission of black and other minorities.

A Nation Divided

Ends versus Means. As a nation we are united on the "ends" of both equal opportunity and affirmative action admission: (1) use of a nondiscriminatory process and (2) increased black and other minority enrollments. We differ dramatically, however, in terms of which end has the highest national priority and the acceptability of the means used in achieving these ends. Those who support equal opportunity admission charge those who support affirmative action admission with employing reverse discrimination, and those who support affirmative action admission charge those who support equal opportunity admission with being "closet racists" or, at best, neoconservatives.

Message or Messenger. More unfortunate, standardized achievement tests used in equal opportunity admissions have become a favorite target for the hostility of those who find the results of such admission decisions to be unacceptable. I believe such hostility is misdirected, for it focuses on the test or the messenger that brings us the bad news rather than on the bad news or the message itself.

The message I am talking about is brutally simple: Until America addresses the problem of a separate and unequal society based on race, we will continue to discriminate against black Americans whenever decisions on college admission are based on standardized achievement tests. In short, the test is not the problem; the problem is our inability or unwillingness as a society to either redress the fundamental problems of poverty, segregation, and discrimination, or to adopt, in the case of access to higher education, affirmative action admissions, which would neutralize the socioeconomic inequities that coincide with race in our society.

Failure of Bakke. The nation hoped that the Supreme Court would resolve the issue once and for all when it ruled on the Bakke case. In a 5-4 decision, it ruled that Bakke's rejection by the University of California's Medical School violated the equal protection clause of the constitution because it used a quota system to select students; however, the court also upheld the principle of affirmative action by saying that race could be an element in evaluating a student's credentials for admission (McCormack, 1978). Thus, despite the initial confusion surrounding the practical implications of the decision, it is generally accepted that the court upheld the legality of moderate affirmative action admission programs. As a result, and despite the prevailing conservative mood throughout the country, existing affirmative action admission programs were not dismantled and the legal groundwork was laid to initiate new such programs when the political mood changed.

Significance of the "Back to Excellence" Movement
on Standardized Testing

Back to Excellence. We are now experiencing a national "back to basics" or "back to excellence" movement. Clearly, for even the casual observer, a change in the American educational system is long overdue and undoubtedly will occur. In the near future, we will see improvement in such areas as teacher preparation, curriculum, discipline, grading standards, and student achievement.

Admission Standards. Four-year colleges, universities, and professional schools have already begun to raise their admission standards. I believe that this will gradually result in a generalized movement away from affirmative action admission to the more traditional equal opportunity admission. Such a movement will entail increased dependence on standardized achievement tests. As a matter of fact, such an increase in the usage of standardized tests has been recommended by the National Commission on Excellence in Education (1983, p. 28).

> Standardized tests of achievement (not to be confused with aptitude tests) should be administered at major transition points from one level of schooling to another and particularly from high school to college or work. The purposes of these tests would be to: (a) certify the student's credentials; (b) identify the need for remedial intervention; and (c) identify the opportunity for advanced or accelerated work. The tests should be administered as part of a nationwide (but not Federal) system of State and local standardized tests. This system should include other diagnostic procedures that assist teachers and students to evaluate student progress.

Thus, a return to excellence will also mean a return to equal opportunity admissions, and if we are not very careful, also a return to an era of minimal black inclusion in higher education.

Significance. If this happens, the message will be clear: Although we recognize that race was once used to exclude blacks and other minorities from institutions of higher education, we are not prepared to use it as a means of guaranteeing their inclusion. This is a tough message but at least it is an honest one. It will also have the salutary effect of forcing black and other concerned Americans to concentrate on the real barriers to their full inclusion into higher education and society.

The Real Problem: Black and Minority Student
Precollege Education

I believe standardized achievement tests are not the problem; they serve only as the messenger bearing ill tidings. Instead of attacking and even attempting to "kill" the messenger for bringing us news we do not want to hear or accept, it would be better to devote our attention to the message and, even more important, to the reasons why it is so bad.

Black Student Performance. For example, despite the gains of the recent past, black student performance on the SAT still trails that of whites. In 1982, the total combined (verbal and mathematical) average scores were 707 for blacks and 927 for whites, a difference of 220 points (Maeroff, 1982). Now, hearing this news, one can do one of three things: (1) wring one's hands and pray for a change; (2) attack the SAT as being racially biased, invalid for measuring future success in college and life, too simplistic, and incapable of measuring such important factors as honesty, leadership abilities, tenacity, or prior social conditions; or (3) identify the reasons why black Americans perform less well than white Americans on the test and then demand that all the resources, both human and material, of our nation be focused on resolving this problem.

I believe that the latter is the only choice that can ultimately resolve the problem. The critical question is whether or not the people of this nation are willing and ready to commit the resources necessary.

Quality of Urban Life. Most black Americans can be found in the poorest sections of the nation's urban centers. Each of these sections, regardless of the city in which it is found, has the following characteristics (Clark, 1970): (1) infant mortality is four times higher than in the rest of the city; (2) life expectancy is ten years shorter; (3) crime is ten times higher; (4) common disease occurs ten times more frequently; (5) unemployment is rampant; (6) homes are in poor condition; and, (7) most important, education is the poorest where schools are the oldest, classrooms are the most crowded, and dropout rates are the highest. Considering these factors, is it not very obvious why black Americans perform less well on achievement tests than whites? Perhaps the most surprising thing is that, despite this enormous handicap, they perform as well as they do. Again, the real question is the willingness of America to solve the underlying problem—social and economic discrimination and segregation based on the historical accident of race.

However, like it or not, standardized achievement tests are the single most powerful tool available for measuring ability accurately, objectively, and with the vital feature of comparability, and when used appropriately, they can be of benefit to all who are directly involved in education.

An Example of the Proper Use of Standardized Testing

New Jersey Basic Skills Program. An excellent recent example of a proper use of achievement testing is the New Jersey Basic Skills Assessment Program, which began in 1977 under the mandate of the New Jersey Board of Higher Education. The program was designed to have two major thrusts: first, to assess the basic skills proficiencies of students entering public colleges in New Jersey, and second, to evaluate the character and effectiveness of the remedial programs at these colleges. To carry out the program, the board created a Basic Skills Council composed of a dozen faculty and staff members from all sectors of higher education in the state. To administer the program, a director, who is a full-time paid staff member, on leave from a college, and a small staff were hired by the Department of Higher Education.

New Jersey Basic Skills Test. With the help of the College Board and under contract with Educational Testing Service, the Basic Skills Council developed the New Jersey College Basic Skills Placement Test (NJCBSPT). The following categories of students are required to take the test after they have been admitted to a public college or university in New Jersey; the test cannot be used as part of the admission process:

1. All full-time and part-time freshmen who are seeking a degree.

2. Any student who does not initially seek a degree but who registers for a course that would result in the accumulation of twelve or more credits.
3. Any freshman transfer student who has not taken the test.

Students enrolled in a bilingual or English as a Second Language (ESL) program may be tested when they have completed such a program. Institutions may require additional categories of freshman students to be tested.

Proficiency Evaluation. The NJCBSPT is a placement test, not a diagnostic instrument, and it has two primary purposes: (1) to help place entering students in appropriate levels of courses from remedial to college level in English and mathematics; and (2) to assess the proficiencies of the entire cohort of students who are entering colleges across the state. The test takes about three and a half hours to administer and includes an essay, four multiple-choice sections, and a series of background questions. Based on their scores, students are grouped into one of three performance categories: lacking proficiency, lacking proficiency in some areas, and proficient in the verbal and mathematical skills tested.

Results. The results of the testing have demonstrated our worst fears: Thousands of students lack proficiency in reading, writing, and mathematics. The problem is pervasive across the state in every high school and is occurring among both recent high school graduates and among students who have been out of school for years. Furthermore, there has been no meaningful change in the test results over the past five years. In addition, the data indicate that successful completion of high school courses does not guarantee proficiency in basic skills.

Initially, publication of the results of the test led to attacks on the test and the way it was used by members of the New Jersey Department of Education, superintendents, principals, teachers, and teacher unions. They, as we should have predicted, attacked the messenger because of their dissatisfaction with the message: Something is dreadfully wrong with our schools.

However, recently due to similar findings by other states,

growing national attention to education and its problems, and new leadership in the New Jersey Department of Education, attention has been refocused on the implications of the findings and the development of several new and exciting initiatives to address some of the causes of the poor performance of so many of our students.

Placement and Program Evaluation. The second major thrust of the program is evaluation of our public colleges' remedial programs. Here the focus has been on six outcome variables: passing rate in remedial courses, attrition rate, grade-point average, the ratio of credits earned to credits attempted, pre- and posttesting, and performance in subsequent college-level courses. While the data are not yet complete for all our colleges, the information collected has led the Basic Skills Council to conclude that remediation can be and is effective for many students. Specifically, students who complete remediation have lower attrition rates, higher grades, and significantly higher posttest scores than students who need remediation but do not take it or complete it.

Major Contributions. Unlike standardized achievement tests used as part of the admission process, the NJCBSPT has made several important contributions while noticeably avoiding the charge of socioeconomic bias. The following are among these contributions:

1. The test has reinforced access while helping to end a revolving door. The Assessment Program has demonstrated that many students with ability to succeed but lacking in proficiency can achieve in college if provided with appropriate remediation. Colleges do not have to choose between limiting access and flunking many students out quickly. Effective testing, placement, and remediation bridges the gap and provides a realistic, viable alternative.

2. Faculty and staff members across the state have worked both within their institution and across colleges, even sectors, to develop effective remedial programs with high standards. The development of a single statewide test has fostered communication by providing a common measure of proficiency and a common base for discussion.

3. Standards have been raised. Colleges have raised the cut scores used in placement, eliminated graduation credit for remediation, and enforced policies requiring remediation for those identified as needing it.

Comparison of the NJCBSPT with Other Standardized Achievement Tests

Although the NJCBSPT has also been the victim of the "messenger/message syndrome," the initial concerns expressed about the test did not for the most part involve charges of racial bias. This difference in public reaction and perception between the NJCBSPT and the other standardized achievement tests used in higher education revolves around the following uses made of the two types of tests:

1. The SAT, GRE, LSAT, and GMAT are used in the admission process while the mandated use of NJCBSPT is restricted to subject proficiency evaluation and course-level placement of admitted students.

2. ETS has historically collected racial, economic, and gender information from those who take the SAT, GRE, LSAT, and GMAT examinations, and it annually reports on the results of these examinations by race and gender. In contrast, to date, neither the Basic Skills Council nor its creator, the New Jersey Board of Higher Education, have requested racial or gender information from those who take the NJCBSPT.

Therefore, since the NJCBSPT plays no role in the determination of who shall and shall not be admitted to institutions of higher education in New Jersey, and since the results of this test are published without racial or gender designation, it poses no immediate threat to many urban and rural black Americans who have been historically victimized by inferior educational preparation in the primary and secondary schools of our nation.

On the contrary, because the New Jersey Board of Higher Education requires that every student in the public sector of higher education who is identified by the NJCBSPT as needing remediation in mathematics or English be enrolled in a collegiate

remedial program, the test has served the salutary role of assist-
ing in the retention of those who have not been adequately prepared academically to benefit from a collegiate curriculum.

Proper Use of Standardized Achievement Tests
in Admission Considerations

Admission Considerations. Does this mean that the use of
standardized achievement tests in collegiate admission decisions
is a misuse of this kind of test? I would argue, No. How they are
used in these decisions is extremely important, however, for this
determines the composition of the student body, and the composition of the student body is directly related to the public image
and mission of the institution, the type of faculty who are attracted to the institution, and ultimately to the composition of
the alumni. Therefore, in deciding who will be admitted, it is
very important to consider a combination of several measures,
differentially weighted to select a student body that meets the
institution's objectives. Consider these five types of measures
with their respective strengths and weaknesses (Willingham and
Breland, 1982).

1. The high school record is highly pertinent because it re-
    flects directly the same type of academic work that is re-
    quired in college, but an element of uncertainty and unfair-
    ness may be involved in comparing records that are often
    not comparable.
2. The admission test provides an objective, common measure
    of academic ability that has general relevance to a wide
    variety of intellectual tasks, but it is a limited measure of
    ability and may underestimate the capability of some stu-
    dents.
3. Personal experience and accomplishment often represent
    real life competence and reflect successful effort that de-
    serves reward, but they may be difficult to assess fairly and
    may not be directly relevant to educational objectives.
4. Background characteristics may be helpful in admitting stu-
    dents whose presence serves institutional objectives, but

they may be irrelevant to other important institutional objectives or otherwise unfair as a basis of preferential treatment.

5. Student interests and goals are especially relevant to effective recruiting and student development, but they may prove capricious and weaken educational programs if overemphasized.

Two-Stage Admission Process. Once these measures and their respective weights have been determined, I would advise the use of a two-stage admission process similar to that described by Manning (1977).

1. The selection from those who apply to the college of those who possess requisite educational credentials and the intellectual abilities considered minimally necessary to pursue and benefit from the academic program of the institution.
2. The selection from this group of a subgroup who collectively will comprise a student body that will foster the institution's image and mission.

In stage one, the critical measures are the high school record and performance on standardized admission tests. The critical measures in stage two are personal qualities.

Summary and Conclusions

Jensen (1980) accurately notes that achievement tests by their very nature measure differences between individuals and thus discriminate. Not only do they discriminate between individuals but also between the statistical averages of different racial, cultural, and socioeconomic subgroups when circumstances cause one or more of the constituent subgroups to perform differently from the others. Thus, if one of the manifestations of racial prejudice against blacks in America is an inferior primary and secondary education, then one would expect them on average to perform less well than their white counterparts on standardized achievement tests used in collegiate admission considerations. To the extent that this results in the exclusion of blacks from higher education, it becomes increasingly an issue of public policy to the nation in general and black Americans in particular.

However, if institutions of higher education would adopt admission procedures similar to those described earlier, and if it were a mission generally shared by most colleges to have a racially diverse student body, then despite the differential performance between blacks and whites on these tests, blacks would not be excluded but affirmatively included in college student bodies.

Unfortunately, the data on black student enrollment does not always confirm that colleges are interested in racially diverse student bodies. The general trend for black enrollment has been one of significant increases in the late sixties and early seventies and then a leveling off from the mid-seventies through the early eighties (Astin, 1982). The vast majority of four-year colleges and universities in the country enroll only about 3 percent minority students.

Also, despite the social gains of the late sixties and early seventies, the plight for most black Americans remains the same, and the quality of their education has deteriorated. Thus, improvement in black student performance on standardized achievement tests will be slow and the gap between their performance and that of white students will continue.

Thus, as we proceed into the decade of the eighties, we can expect continued attacks on "messengers," for unfortunately there seems to be no change in sight in the message itself.

References

Astin, A. W. *Minorities in American Higher Education: Recent Trends, Current Prospects, and Recommendations.* San Francisco: Jossey-Bass, 1982.

Clark, R. *Crime in America.* New York: Simon & Schuster, 1970.

Jensen, A. R. *Bias in Mental Testing.* New York: The Free Press, 1980.

McCormack, W. "The Bakke Decision: Implications for Higher Education Admissions." A Report of the ACE-AALS Committee on Bakke. Washington, D.C.: American Council on Education and Association of American Law Schools, 1978.

Maeroff, G. "Minority Groups Played Key Role in Rise of Scores in College Exams." *New York Times,* October 14, 1982.

Manning, W. H. "The Pursuit of Fairness in Admissions to Higher Education." In Carnegie Council on Policy Studies in Higher Education, W. M. Manning, W. W. Willingham, and H. M. Breland and Associates, *Selective Admissions in Higher Education: Comment and Recommendations and Two Reports.* San Francisco: Jossey-Bass, 1977.

Nairn, A., and Associates. *The Reign of ETS: The Corporation that Makes Up Minds.* Washington, D.C.: Ralph Nader, 1980.

National Advisory Commission on Civil Disorders. *Report.* Washington, D.C.: U.S. Government Printing Office, 1968.

National Commission on Excellence in Education. *A Nation at Risk: The Imperative for Educational Reform: A Report to the Nation and the Secretary of Education.* Washington, D.C.: United States Department of Education, 1983.

Williams, R. L. "Abuses and Misuses in Testing Black Children." *Counseling Psychologist,* 1971, *2,* 62–77.

Willingham, W. W., and Breland, H. M. *Personal Qualities and College Admissions.* New York: College Entrance Examination Board, 1982.

8

Legal Constraints on Test Use in the Schools

Donald N. Bersoff

Testing is now a regulated industry. In fact, it may seem that the courts, Congress, and the state legislators control the practice of educational testing rather than the scientific and professional organizations one assumes would serve that function. At one time, of course, the work of academic and applied psychometricians went virtually unexamined by the law, but as the use of tests increased in the United States, so did their potential for causing legally cognizable injury to test takers. As a result, there is probably no current activity performed by psychologists so closely scrutinized and regulated by the legal system as testing.

This chapter is devoted to an examination of this phenomenon. To make this presentation more manageable, the chapter will focus on one particular injury and one setting in which tests are administered. Thus, I will limit my analysis to the claim that psychological tests administered in the public schools are tools of discrimination that deny full realization of the rights of racial and ethnic minorities and the handicapped.

To better understand what will follow, it may be helpful to understand the basic theories that permit the legal system to inquire about what is fundamentally a scientific and professional activity. The courts are traditionally wary of interfering with the discretion of trained experts, especially in those areas in which they concede lack of specialized knowledge. And, few fields of endeavor are more arcane and unknowable than measurement and evaluation. However, when the activities of psychologists directly and sharply implicate fundamental values protected by the constitution, the courts, as ultimate interpreters of its content, have found it appropriate to intervene.

Two basic constitutional values relevant to those who construct, use, interpret, and take tests appear in the fifth and fourteenth amendments. Generally, those amendments serve as barriers to thoughtless and arbitrary actions by local, county, state, and federal officials (the fifth amendment pertains to the federal government; the fourteenth to other governmental entities). The two most important concepts embodied in those amendments are equal protection and due process. Under the equal protection clause, governments are forbidden to treat persons who are similarly situated differently unless there is a supportable reason for so doing. And, when special groups of persons are affected by the state's action, the courts will scrutinize that action even more closely. For example, when the state has deliberately acted to the disadvantage of racial and ethnic minorities, it must prove that it has a compelling or overriding need to do so. This is because these groups have been "saddled with such disabilities or [have been] subjected to such a history of purposeful unequal treatment, or relegated to such a position of political powerlessness as to command extraordinary protection from the majoritarian political process" (*San Antonio Independent School District* v. *Rodriguez,* 1973, p. 28). The result, when courts apply this "strict scrutiny" test, is almost invariably against the government.

The due process clause forbids the government from denying persons life, liberty, or property without a legitimate reason and without providing some meaningful and impartial forum to prevent arbitrary deprivations of those protected interests. Both property and liberty interests have been broadly defined by the Supreme Court. Property interests include any government-created entitlements such as tenure, licensure to practice one's profession, or access to public education. Liberty includes not only freedom from involuntary incarceration in a prison or commitment to a mental institution. It can also encompass the right to privacy, personal security, and reputation. Thus, for example, the constitution prevents governmental institutions from unilateral, unsupportable, and stigmatizing labeling—"official branding," Justice Douglas once called it—of persons as handicapped or mentally ill. What procedures due process may require under any given set of circumstances begin with a determination of the precise nature of the government function as well as the potential entitlement that will be lost as a result of the governmental action. Although the precise contours of due process change with the nature of the interest at stake, at bottom the clause requires fundamental fairness when the government deals with persons within its jurisdiction.

In addition to these constitutional guarantees, a whole litany of federal and state statutory protections may be invoked to challenge the inappropriate use of tests, not only in the public sector but in private industry as well. Together, these enactments provide extensive armamentaria for potential plaintiffs.

With this background, I will now turn to some of the most important examples of challenges to tests in the public schools. In doing so, I will concentrate on challenges to individually administered intelligence tests and to group administered minimal competency examinations. (For a fuller discussion of legal issues related to educational testing, including the early history of litigation, see, for example, Bersoff, 1979, 1981, 1982, 1983a, 1983b, 1983c; Hartshorne, 1978; Heller, Holtzman and Messick, 1982; Sherman and Robinson, 1982; Wigdor and Garner, 1982.)

Individual Intelligence Tests: Landmark Cases

The decade from 1971 to 1980 brought the most severe challenge to the use of individual intelligence scales as the result of federal court decisions in San Francisco, *Larry P.* v. *Riles* (1979), and Chicago, *PASE (Parents in Action on Special Education)* v. *Hannon* (1980). In analysis, style, reasoning, and outcome, these two decisions are diametrically opposed. Both cases represent the continuing opposition to ability tests that began with *Hobson* v. *Hansen* (1967), in which minorities questioned the constitutionality of relying on group tests to place children in ability tracks. *Hobson,* when read in its entirety, represents the justified condemnation of rigid, poorly conceived classification practices that damage the educational opportunities of minority children. But also falling under disapprobation in *Hobson* was the use of group assessment devices as the primary determinant for tracking. In *Larry P.* and *PASE,* the focus shifted to the more time-honored instruments for measuring intelligence—the Wechsler Intelligence Scale for Children (WISC), the WISC-Revised (WISC-R), and the Stanford-Binet Intelligence Scale—and the challenge was solely to the placement of children in self-contained classes for the educable mentally retarded (EMR).

In *Larry P.,* the court, basing its analysis primarily on the constitution, the 1964 Civil Rights Act, the Rehabilitation Act of 1973, and the Education for All Handicapped Children Act of 1975 (Public Law 94-142), ruled in favor of the minority plaintiffs and against the California State Department of Education. Interpreting the nondiscriminatory provisions of the Rehabilitation Act and Public Law 94-142, particularly regulations requiring that assessment instruments be "validated for the specific purpose for which they are used" (34 C.F.R. Sec. 104.35; 34 C.F.R. Sec. 300.532), the court mandated the state to meet the following standards before it could use intelligence scales:

1. Tests would have to yield the same pattern of scores when administered to different groups of students.
2. Tests would have to yield approximately equal means for all subgroups included in the standardization sample.
3. Tests would have to be correlated with relevant criterion measures; that is, IQ scores of black children would have to be correlated with classroom performance.

Given these criteria, it is unlikely that any of the currently used intelligence tests are valid, which casts doubt on the continued utility of traditional evaluations using psychology's storehouse of standardized ability tests.

Because the tests were the primary basis for placement in

California's EMR programs (harshly condemned by the court), because black students were highly overrepresented in these programs, and because they did significantly less well on these tests than did their white counterparts, the court felt it necessary to confront the explanations for disparities in IQ test performance between minority and majority pupils. The court quickly rejected any notion of inherent inferiority in black children and found socioeconomic explanations (on which the state primarily relied) unpersuasive.

The court then examined the hypothesis that cultural bias in the tests was the most cogent explanation for the disparities. The court noted that versions of the Stanford-Binet and Wechsler scales prior to the 1970s had been developed using only white children in the process of deriving norms against which all children would be measured. That these tests had been restandardized in the early 1970s to include a representative proportion of black children did not satisfy the court that they were valid for culturally different groups: "Mixing the populations without more does not eliminate any preexisting bias" (p. 957). The process failed to yield data that could be used to compare black and white children's performance on particular items.

In addition to standardization problems, the court identified two other indexes of cultural bias. First, to the extent that black children were more likely to be exposed to nonstandard English, they would be handicapped in the verbal component of intelligence tests. Second, the court averred that certain items were inherently unfair to black children from culturally different environments when viewed from the perspective of the scoring criteria offered in the examiners' manual. The court concluded that "to the extent that a 'black culture' exists and translates the phenomenon of intelligence into skills and knowledge untested by the standardized intelligence tests, those tests cannot measure the capabilities of black children" (p. 960). The court charged that the tests were never designed to eliminate bias against black children and blamed test developers and users for assuming "in effect that black children were less 'intelligent' than whites" (pp. 956-957).

After finding for the plaintiffs, all that was left for the

court was to forge proper remedies. In doing so it recognized the genuine changes initiated by California during the course of litigation and the complexity and risk of judicial interference in the administration of education. It also did not want its condemnation of intelligence tests to be seen as the final judgment on the scientific validity of such devices. But these concerns did not dissuade the court from holding the state responsible for its failure to properly assess and educate black children and from fashioning remedies to halt both test abuse and disproportionate enrollment of blacks in EMR classes.

The court permanently enjoined the state from using any standardized intelligence tests to identify black children for EMR placement without first securing approval from the court. The state board of education would have to petition the court after determining that the tests they sought to use were not racially or culturally discriminatory, that they would be administered in a nondiscriminatory manner, and that they had been validated for the purpose of placing black children in EMR classes. The petition would have to be supported by statistical evidence submitted under oath and by certification that public hearings had been held concerning the proposed tests.

The decision, over the objection of the California State Board of Education, was appealed by Defendant Riles to the Ninth Circuit Court of Appeals. In November 1981, the appellate tribunal had heard the case, and rendered its decision in January 1984, affirming the lower court's decision in all its essential respects.

Almost nine months to the day after Judge Peckham issued his opinion in *Larry P.,* Judge Grady, a federal court judge in Illinois, rendered his decision in *PASE* v. *Hannon* (1980). While the facts, issues, claims, and witnesses were very similar to *Larry P.,* the analysis and outcome could not have been more different. Rather than ruling that the tests in question were culturally biased, as did Judge Peckham, Judge Grady held "that the WISC, WISC-R, and Stanford-Binet tests, when used in conjunction with the statutorily mandated ['other criteria'] for determining an appropriate educational program for a child [under Pub. L. 94-142] . . . do not discriminate against black children in the Chicago public schools. Defendants are complying with the statutory mandate" (*PASE* v. *Hannon,* 1980, p. 883).

While Judge Peckham frequently cited the opinions of behavioral science experts, Judge Grady was significantly less influenced by such testimony. He felt it imperative to examine the tests themselves so he could judge whether the claim of cultural bias could be sustained. Thus, in a startling and extraordinary maneuver, he proceeded to cite each question on the Wechsler and Stanford-Binet scales, along with every acceptable response, in an attempt to determine which, in his estimation, were culturally biased. The result of this analysis was the judgment that only eight items on the WISC/WISC-R and one item on the Stanford-Binet were suspect or actually biased.

If the tests were not culturally biased, then, what was the explanation for the significant mean differences between white and black children's IQ scores? Like the parties in *Larry P.,* both the plaintiffs and defendants in *PASE* rejected a genetic theory: "There is no dispute . . . about the equality of innate intellectual capacity. Defendants assert no less strongly than plaintiffs that there are no genetic differences in mental capacity" (*PASE* v. *Hannon,* 1980, p. 877). Unlike the court in *Larry P.,* where Judge Peckham had rejected a socioeconomic explanation, Judge Grady found that argument persuasive. Accepting the arguments of the school system's witnesses that the acquisition of intellectual skills is greatly affected by a child's early intellectual stimulation, the court reasoned:

> Defendant's explanation of the I.Q. difference, that it is caused by socio-economic factors . . . is consistent with other circumstances not accounted for by plaintiff's theory of cultural bias. . . . Plaintiffs' theory . . . simply ignores the fact that black children perform differently from each other on the tests. It also fails to explain the fact that some black children perform better than most whites [p. 878].

With that, the court concluded that the plaintiffs had failed to prove their contention that the intelligence tests were

culturally unfair to black children. Even if they were, the court
believed that still would not make the assessment process
biased. Judge Grady read Pub. L. 94-142's prohibition against
single measures and its requirement of nondiscriminatory assessment as meaning that the entire psychoeducational evaluation,
when viewed as a whole, had to be nonbiased. A single procedure, by itself, could be discriminatory without condemning the
entire system as invalid for placing minority children in EMR
programs. The court reasoned that multiple procedures assured
that results from the intelligence test would be interpreted in
the light of other evaluation devices and information sources.

The court in *PASE,* therefore, viewed the placement process as a protective device against misclassification, in contrast
to the court in *Larry P.,* which concentrated on an analysis of
the tests. Judge Peckham found California's system of assessment sound in theory but condemned it in practice, finding that
testing continued to loom as the most important determinant
of EMR placement. Judge Grady scrutinized the process in Chicago and concluded that referral, screening, multidisciplinary
evaluation, and the staff conference helped insure that misclassification did not occur. In fact, he found that for all subranges
within the EMR classification scheme, fewer children were ultimately labeled as retarded than would have been the case based
on their IQ score alone. Although the court conceded that some
children were misplaced, it rejected the hypothesis that erroneous placements were due to racial bias in the intelligence tests.
(However, for research that casts serious doubt on this analysis
and concludes that IQ is the critical causal variable in the placement, see Berk, Bridges, and Shih, 1981.)

But what of Judge Peckham's decision in *Larry P.?* Judge
Grady's reference to *Larry P.* occupied a bit less than one page
of his long opinion, and he virtually rejected its persuasiveness
out of hand. He concluded that Judge Peckham's analysis never
attacked what Judge Grady considered the threshold question—
whether the tests were in fact biased. Judge Grady believed that
one could not arrive at a proper decision concerning the plaintiffs' claims in either case without examining the issue of test
bias in detail. As for the California court's ultimate decision,

Judge Grady merely said, "the witnesses and the arguments which persuaded Judge Peckham have not persuaded me" (*PASE*, p. 882).

The plaintiff school children appealed Judge Grady's decision. Ironically, Chicago's new school board voluntarily decided to end individual intelligence testing for EMR placement as part of a schoolwide desegregation plan, thereby making the appeal unnecessary from the plaintiffs' perspective. The case is currently entangled in procedural maneuvers and an ultimate decision on appeal may never be reached.

Minimum Competency Testing

Although the psycholegal aspects of minimum competency testing programs have been the subject of some comment (for example, Lerner, 1981; Lewis, 1979; Lynch, 1982; Madaus and McDonagh, 1979; McClung, 1979), the movement has not yet received all the attention it deserves. In part, it may be that challenges to individual intelligence tests, which more directly affect the interests of professional psychologists and involve threats to one of psychology's most hallowed contributions, have preoccupied the attention of the field. However, the use of competency tests to determine eligibility for graduation and/or diploma affects decidedly more test takers than does the use of individual intelligence tests for placement in classes for the educably mentally retarded. With the number of states now using minimal competency tests changing rapidly, it is difficult to be precise about the extent to which these tests are administered, but about 80 percent of the states now have some kind of competency examination and about 50 percent use the test as a prerequisite for the award of a diploma (Lerner, 1981; Tuttle, 1980). Thus, legal challenges to minimum competency tests may have more national significance than cases like *Larry P.* and *PASE*.

The first, and perhaps most important, case challenging minimum competency tests in the federal courts is *Debra P. v. Turlington* (1979; 1981; 1983), a class action on behalf of high school seniors in Florida who had failed or would later fail the state's self-styled Functional Literacy Test. Passing the test was a condition precedent to receipt of a diploma; those who ultimately failed the test would receive only a certificate of completion if they met other requirements for graduation. The plaintiffs contended that the test was racially biased, instituted without adequate notice that passing it would be necessary if the student wished a diploma, and would be used to resegregate the state's public schools through the use of remedial classes for those who failed the exam. Among the legal theories used to challenge use of the test were the now familiar claims that it violated the equal protection and due process clauses of the constitution and Title VI of the 1964 Civil Rights Act.

By the time the lawsuit was filed, the test had been administered three times with black students uniformly failing at a disproportionately high rate. That finding, coupled with the fact that Florida's school systems were segregated by law until 1971, had a significant impact on the trial court's initial decision. The court acknowledged that the state had a legitimate interest in implementing a procedure to evaluate established educational objectives, but the court attributed the disparate impact on blacks to their inferior education in dual school systems. Thus, as in *Larry P.*, the court concluded that "race more than any other factor, including socioeconomic status, is a predictor of success on the test" (*Debra P. v. Turlington*, 1979, pp. 256–257), the result of which was to perpetuate past purposeful discrimination. In that light, the court held that the use of the tests to deny diplomas violated the equal protection clause and Title VI.

The court also agreed that the test violated due process. The students' expectation of a diploma was seen as a property interest protected by the fourteenth amendment. The labeling of those who failed the test as functional illiterates and their receipt of a certificate of completion instead of a diploma was seen as adverse stigma infringing on the liberty component of due process. As a result, the court held that notice to students less than two years before implementation of the diploma sanction was inadequate to protect those constitutional interests. Such limited notice was insufficient to prepare for a statewide test for which there was no statewide curriculum. However, the court cursorily brushed aside allegations that the test contained racially biased items.

Most important for present purposes was the court's evaluation of the validity of the test itself. The test was a criterion-referenced assessment of mastery in twenty-four skill objectives in reading, writing, arithmetic, and the solution of practical problems. Using as a basis for decision the *Standards for Educational and Psychological Tests* (APA, AERA, NCME, 1974), the court held that the test was both content and construct valid, that is, that the test items adequately measured skill objectives and matched consensual definitions of functional illiteracy. Thus, while the timing of the test was condemned, the test itself was not.

Nevertheless, because of the infirmity as to notice, the end result was that the use of the test as a diploma-granting device was enjoined until the 1982-83 school year, when all students in the state had access to a complete twelve-year cycle of desegregated education. But the state was not precluded from using the test to assist in the identification and remediation of those who could not meet minimum skill objectives.

Both sides appealed the decision. While the fifth circuit concurred with the judgment below it on almost all grounds, that is, that the test was rationally related to a valid state interest and that it possessed construct validity, it disagreed on one major ground. It called the lower court's finding that the test was content valid "clearly erroneous" (*Debra P.* v. *Turlington,* 1981, p. 405). In the educational context, it defined content validity to mean curricular validity: "We believe that the state administered a test that was, at least on the record before us, fundamentally unfair in that it *may* have covered matters not taught in the schools of the state" (p. 404) [italics in original]. It conceded that the test was probably a good match of what students should know but concluded that there was no evidence that it measured what they had an opportunity to learn. As a result, the court of appeals remanded the case to the trial court to develop a record that would provide proof that the "test administered measures what was actually taught in the schools of

Florida" (p. 405). If the test failed to meet the curricular validity criterion, it would run afoul of the constitution's requirement that state-imposed requirements infringing on protectible
interests shall not be arbitrary or irrational.

In accordance with the court of appeals order, the trial
court heard testimony on the issue of instructional validity
early in 1983 and issued its opinion on May 4th. Both sides presented highly reputable and nationally known experts whose
names would be instantly familiar to this audience. And, as in
Larry P. and *PASE,* the witnesses were sharply divided in their
conclusions. The court thus recognized that "the resolution of
the instructional validity issue depends on whose experts are believed and on what sort of proof is required" (*Debra P.* v. *Turlington,* 1983, p. 183). It also acknowledged that issues concerning curricular validity and minimal competency testing
generally "are relatively new and highly controversial subjects
which seem to have polarized the educational community" (p.
183). Finally, it conceded that "instructional validity is an elusive concept [that] . . . strikes at the heart of the learning and
teaching process" (p. 184). After considering the conflicting
testimony in light of constitutional requirements, the court concluded that Florida's functional literacy examination was "cur-
ricularly valid," that is, that the test covered what was actually
taught in most, if not all, of the state's schools (p. 185). In addition, it upheld the use of the test because students were given
five chances to pass the test and remedial help was offered to
those who had failed. In sum, it held that:

> The defendants have carried their burden of
> proving by a preponderance of the evidence that
> the SSAT-II [the test at issue] is instructionally
> valid and therefore constitutional. Although the in-
> struction offered in all of the classrooms of all the
> districts might not be ideal, students are neverthe-
> less afforded an adequate opportunity to learn the
> skills tested on the SSAT-II before it is used as a
> diploma sanction [p. 186].

Debra P., of course, is not the only case concerning challenges by minorities and the handicapped to minimal competency tests (see *Anderson* v. *Banks,* 1981; *Board of Education of Northport-East Northport Union Free School District* v. *Ambach,* 1982; *Brookhart* v. *Illinois State Board of Education,* 1982, 1983). By and large these decisions, under facts that assume that the tests are given fairly, with proper notice, and to students who have completed a full cycle of desegregated education, have supported their use. However, the case law in this area is still developing, and it is difficult to discern generalizable principles. Often the decisions have failed to address significant issues. For example, in some jurisdictions students are dichotomized as either literate or illiterate and may be denied the extremely significant credential of a diploma on the basis of one test. Both *Larry P.* and *PASE* agreed that special education placement and labeling must be grounded on information gleaned from a multifaceted assessment. Arguably, the interests at stake in minimal competency testing are greater than those in the IQ-testing cases. Yet, the courts have never prohibited school systems from applying the diploma sanction on the basis of a single test score, although the appellate court in *Brookhart* intimated it might if it was found that the minimal competency test score was the sole criterion for graduation. The one identifiable trend is toward the use of a curricular validity criterion to judge whether minimal competency tests will pass legal muster. To withstand scrutiny, it is becoming clear that such tests must measure what students have been taught. This standard is very much like that in cases challenging employment tests in which the courts have required some evidence of job relatedness.

Some Lessons and Comments

The involvement of the legal system in psychological testing in the public schools is not over. Even this abbreviated review should indicate that legal scrutiny of testing is both a present and future reality. It is unfortunate, then, that many judicial decisions in this area are less than intelligently reasoned and psychometrically accurate.

For example, both of the decisions involving individual intelligence testing—*Larry P.* and *PASE*—and to some extent those involving minimal competence tests have rested on the respective courts' resolutions of claims of cultural bias. The permanent injunction in *Larry P.* was based, in large part, on the conclusion that the tests were invalid for minority children because of bias. The strength of the opinion, therefore, depends almost entirely on the correctness of this finding, which, I believe, possesses unfortunate infirmities. In like manner, the outcome in *PASE* is sustainable only if the finding of nondiscrimination in the challenged tests is correct. The method by which Judge Grady reached that judgment is embarrassingly unsophisticated and ingenuous.

Larry P. defines an unbiased test as one that yields "the same pattern of scores when administered to different groups of people" (p. 955). Most test developers would, I think, agree that such a definition is psychometrically unsound. Tests are fair when they predict with equal accuracy, not with equal results, for all groups. The court's definition "eliminates a priori any possibility of real group differences on various psychological traits" (Schmidt and Hunter, 1974, p. 1). Although the court based its decision on the finding that the tests were culturally biased, empirical support for its conclusions consumed only one of seventy pages. Moreover, the court's determination that the tests contain items biased against poor black children is not uniformly accepted, and there are data suggesting that whatever discrimination exists in tests is not the result of content bias. While criticism of Judge Peckham's analysis does not imply that his conclusion is incorrect or that there is support for alternative hypotheses concerning disparities between black and white mean IQ scores, what has been found with regard to standardized group tests generally (Flaugher, 1978), or individual intelligence tests specifically (Reschly, 1980; Reynolds, 1982; Sandoval, 1979), does not support the court's conclusions (see also Bersoff, 1982).

If Judge Peckham's analysis is scanty and faulty, Judge Grady's can best be described as naive; at worst it is unintelligent and completely empty of empirical substance. It represents a single person's subjective and personal opinion cloaked in the authority of judicial robes. If submitted as a study to one of psychology's more respected refereed journals rather than masquerading as a legal opinion, it would have been summarily rejected as an experiment whose sample size and lack of objectivity stamped it as unworthy of publication. The court's decision amply supports Reschly's (1980) conclusion that with regard to item bias on individually administered intelligence tests, "subjective judgments appear to be unreliable and invalid in terms of empirical analysis" (p. 127). Much of the data that now exist are judgmental and speculative.

What makes Judge Grady's opinion interesting, if not precedent setting, is that it contains the questions on and correct answers to the Wechsler and Stanford-Binet scales. So even though he upheld the tests as valid, his decision, to a far greater extent that Judge Peckham's, may have the effect of invalidating the tests as they are presently used. The security of these instruments has been seriously compromised, if not destroyed.

My complaints about the judiciary, however, should not deflect responsibility from psychologists. It may be legitimate to place at least part of the fault for the current and continuing confusion concerning tests on psychologists themselves. One of the more intriguing aspects of Judge Grady's decision in *PASE* v. *Hannon* was his almost utter rejection of the testimony of expert psychologists who testified either for the black children challenging the IQ tests or for the school system seeking to defend them. In a quote that deserves some thought he said:

> None of the witnesses in this case has so impressed me with his or her credibility or expertise that I would feel secure in basing a decision simply on his or her opinion. In some instances, I am satisfied that the opinions expressed are more the result of doctrinaire commitment to a preconceived idea than they are the result of scientific inquiry. I need something more than the conclusions of witnesses in order to arrive at my own conclusion [1980, p. 836].

Several years ago Cronbach (1975) warned psychologists

involved in testing issues not to be advocates. But far too often they have testified for one side or the other. Although psychologists perform a valuable service when they testify as expert witnesses, they should be aware that their data, interpretations, and opinions will be tested in the crucible of courtroom cross-examination whose very purpose is to destroy credibility and evoke evidence of bias on the part of the expert. Whereas the distillation of that process may yield testimony of great consequence and weight to the court, it can be highly anxiety-provoking for the psychologist who acts as an injudicious advocate, pleading for a position, rather than as a cautious, neutral scientist presenting data in an even-handed manner.

Finally, although recent litigation and legislation directly affect the continued administration of psychological testing in educational settings, my contention is that what appears to be an antitesting movement in the courts and in the legislature is not an antitesting movement at all. The legal system's scrutiny of testing has been evoked, in major part, by its concern that our society undo the effects of *de jure* segregation and discrimination against racial and ethnic minorities and the handicapped. The cases I have discussed flow inexorably from the Supreme Court's ringing declarations in *Brown* v. *Board of Education* (1954) ending state-imposed segregation in the public schools. These modern cases are simply renewed claims by minorities for the fulfillment of the meaning of the fourteenth amendment's equal protection clause. They reflect the most recent challenges to practices that are perceived as attempts to continue, in a more sophisticated manner, the racial and ethnic separation more blatantly used in the early 1950s and 1960s by educational institutions.

Although the legal system has often been misguided and naive in its judgments about testing, there are at least three benefits from the increased involvement of courts and legislatures in psychologists' testing practices. First, it has made the profession, as well as society in general, more sensitive to racial and cultural differences and to how apparently innocent and benign practices may perpetuate discrimination. Second, it has alerted psychologists to the fact that they will be held responsible for their conduct. To protect the rights of test takers, to safeguard their own integrity, and, in the long run, to serve the legitimate goals of their employers, psychologists must examine their practices, their interpretations, and their ultimate recommendations. Finally, the attack on psychological testing has accelerated the search for both improved and alternative means of assessment so that what is said about examinees more validly and truly depicts their perceptions of themselves and how they function in all spheres of life. In this light, the intense and searching examination that psychological assessment has received from the legal system should be viewed as both salutary and welcome.

References

American Psychological Association, American Educational Research Association, and National Council on Measurement in Education. *Standards for Educational and Psychological Tests*. Washington, D.C.: American Psychological Association, 1974.

Anderson v. *Banks,* 520 F. Supp. 472 (N.D. Ga. 1981).

Berk, R., Bridges, W., and Shih, A. "Does IQ Really Matter? A Study of the Use of IQ Scores for the Tracking of the Mentally Retarded." *American Sociological Review,* 1981, *46,* 58-71.

Bersoff, D. "Regarding Psychologists Testily: Legal Regulation of Psychological Assessment in the Public Schools." *Maryland Law Review,* 1979, *39,* 27-120.

Bersoff, D. "Testing and the Law." *American Psychologist,* 1981, *36,* 1047-1056.

Bersoff, D. "*Larry P.* and *PASE*: Judicial Report Cards on the Validity of Individual Intelligence Tests." In T. Kratochwill (Ed.), *Advances in School Psychology*. Vol. 2. Hillsdale, N.J.: Erlbaum, 1982.

Bersoff, D. "Social and Legal Influences in Test Development and Usage." In B. Plake and S. Hansen (Eds.), *Buros-Nebraska Symposium on Measurement and Testing*. Lincoln: University of Nebraska Press, 1983a.

Bersoff, D. "Children as Participants in Psychoeducational Assessment." In G. Melton, G. Koocher, and M. Saks (Eds.), *Developmental Factors in Competence to Consent.* New York:
Plenum, 1983b.

Bersoff, D. "Regarding Psychologists Testily: The Legal Regulation of Psychological Assessment." In J. Schierer and B.
Hammonds (Eds.), *Master Lecture Series.* Vol. II: *Psychology
and the Law.* Washington, D.C.: American Psychological Association, 1983c.

*Board of Education of Northport-East Northport Union Free
School District* v. *Ambach,* 458 N.Y.S.2d 680 (A.D. 1982).

Brookhart v. *Illinois State Board of Education,* 534 F. Supp.
725 (C.D. Ill. 1982), *rev'd,* 697 F.2d 179 (7th Cir. 1983).

Brown v. *Board of Education,* 347 U.S. 483 (1954).

Cronbach, L. "Five Decades of Public Controversy over Mental
Testing." *American Psychologist,* 1975, *30,* 1-14.

Debra P. v. *Turlington,* 474 F. Supp. 244 (M.D. Fla. 1979),
affirmed in part and remanded in part, 644 F.2d 397 (5th
Cir. 1981), *on remand,* 564 F. Supp. 177 (M.D. Fla. 1983).

Flaugher, R. "The Many Definitions of Test Bias." *American
Psychologist,* 1978, *33,* 671-679.

Hartshorne, N. (Ed.). *Educational Measurement and the Law.*
Princeton, N.J.: Educational Testing Service, 1978.

Heller, K., Holtzman, W., and Messick, S. *Placing Children in
Special Education: A Strategy for Equity.* Washington, D.C.:
National Academy Press, 1982.

Hobson v. *Hansen,* 269 F. Supp. 401 (D.D.C. 1967), *affirmed
sub nom. Smuck* v. *Hobson,* 408 F.2d 175 (D.C. Cir. 1969).

Larry P. v. *Riles,* 495 F. Supp. 926 (N.D. Cal. 1979), appeal
docketed, No. 80-4027 (9th Cir. Jan. 19, 1980).

Lerner, B. "The Minimum Competence Testing Movement: Social, Scientific and Legal Implications." *American Psychologist,* 1981, *36,* 1057-1066.

Lewis, P. "Certifying Functional Literacy: Competency Testing
and Implications for Due Process and Equal Educational Opportunity." *Journal of Law and Education,* 1979, *8,* 145-
163.

Lynch, D. "Education Law." *Syracuse Law Review,* 1982, *33,*
203-233.

McClung, M. "Competency Testing Programs: Legal and Educational Issues." *Fordham Law Review,* 1979, *47,* 651-702.

Madaus, G. and McDonagh, J. "Minimum Competency Testing: Unexamined Assumptions and Unexplored Negative Outcomes." In Roger T. Lennon (Ed.), *New Directions for Testing and Measurement: Impactive Changes on Measurement,* no. 3. San Francisco: Jossey-Bass, 1979.

PASE (Parents in Action on Special Education) v. *Hannon,* 506 F. Supp. 831 (N.D. Ind. 1980).

Reschly, D. "Psychological Evidence in the *Larry P.* Opinion: A Case of Right Problem—Wrong Solution?" *School Psychology Review,* 1980, *9,* 123-135.

Reynolds, C. "The Problem of Bias in Psychological Assessment." In C. Reynolds and T. Gutkin (Eds.), *The Handbook of School Psychology.* New York: Wiley, 1982.

San Antonio Independent School District v. *Rodriguez,* 411 U.S. 1 (1973).

Sandoval, J. "The WISC-R and Internal Evidence of Test Bias and Minority Groups. *Journal of Counseling and Clinical Psychology,* 1979, *47,* 919-927.

Schmidt, F., and Hunter, J. "Racial and Ethnic Bias in Psychological Tests: Divergent Implications of Two Definitions of Test Bias." *American Psychologist,* 1974, *29,* 1-8.

Sherman, S., and Robinson, N. (Eds.). *Ability Testing of Handicapped People: Dilemma for Government, Science and the Public.* Washington, D.C.: National Academy Press, 1982.

Tuttle, S. "Education and the Law: Functional Literacy Program—a Matter of Timing." *Stetson Law Review,* 1980, *10,* 125-139.

Wigdor, A., and Garner, W. (Eds.). *Ability Testing: Uses, Consequences, and Controversies.* Washington, D.C.: National Academy Press, 1982.

Index

127

Index

133

Tests and testing *(continued)*:
  proper use of, 7-10, 98-101, 102-103
  and public policy, 2-5
  public stake in, 1-11
  regulation of, 107-109
  in schools, 47-67, 107-125
  standards for, 13-46
  state-administered, 5
  as tool, 22-23
  utility of, 53-54
  validation of, 18, 24, 43, 117-118
  value of standardized, 59-67
Topping, C., 49, 57
Tuttle, S., 115, 125

V

Validation:
  in court case, 117-118
  issue of, 18, 24, 43

Virginia, educational system in, 4

W

Waley, A., 1
Wechsler Intelligence Scale for Children (WISC), 110, 111, 112, 113, 121
Wechsler Intelligence Scale for Children-Revised (WISC-R), 110, 111, 112, 113, 121
Weikart, D. P., 55, 57
Wigdor, A., 109, 125
Wiley, D., 62
Williams, R. L., 91, 105
Willingham, W. W., 76, 89, 102-103, 105
Winter, M., 49, 57
Wirtz, W., 62, 66
Wise, D. A., 73, 89
Wu Ch'êng'ên, 1n